Dante Rossetti:
117 Masterpieces

By Maria Tsaneva

First Edition

*****

I0477315

Dante Rossetti: 117 Masterpieces
*****

Foreword

Dante Gabriel Rossetti was an English poet, illustrator, painter and translator. He founded the Pre-Raphaelite Brotherhood in 1848 with William Holman Hunt and John Everett Millais, and was later to be the main inspiration for a second generation of artists and writers influenced by the movement, most notably William Morris and Edward Burne-Jones. His work also influenced the European Symbolists and was a major precursor of the Aesthetic movement.

Rossetti's art was characterized by its sensuality and its medieval revivalism. His early poetry was influenced by John Keats. He is considered one of the most unconventional painters of the 19th century. Through his methods, he distinguished himself from the Pre-Raphaelite movement; he showed no interest on the exact representation of details, avoided complicated backgrounds, and tended away from landscapes. He hence chose primarily mythological or literary motives, though with no narrative moment.

Gabriel Charles Dante Rossetti, usually recognized as Dante Gabriel Rossetti, was born in London. His father was an Italian who had established in England.

Even as a child, Rossetti showed imaginative ability, and in view of that was sent to learn drawing under John Sell Cotman, Soon later he entered the Royal Academy and in 1848, commenced working in the studio of Ford Madox Brown, for the duration of which time he began to demonstrate himself a painter of distinctive personality, while at the same time he complete his first essays in translating Italian writing into English and became well-known among his friends as a bard of extraordinary promise.

For the meantime, on the other hand, Rossetti was actually more involved in painting quite than writing, and shortly after leaving Brown's studio he brought about a outstanding event in the history of English painting by start the Pre-Raphaelite Brotherhood, a organization consisting of seven members, whose essential intend was to give exactly and accurately every separate thing figured in their pictures. Leaving his father's home in 1849, Rossetti went to reside at Chatham Place in London, and throughout the next ten years his activity as a painter was colossal.

The year 1860 was outstanding one in his career, as it marked his marriage ceremony to Eleanor Siddal. The love between the couple was unusually obsessive. Nevertheless, Eleanor Siddal died in 1862. The loss of his wife preyed upon him steadily; he was suffering by sleeplessness and, in result, began to take sporadic doses of the drug chloral. Step by step, this practice developed into a habit, and it before long became clear that his death was about to happen unless he gave up his dependence to the drug.

He died April 9, 1882, and was interred in the cemetery there.

Rossetti had a marked tendency for mysticism in a range of forms. A faith in the option of communicating with the dead may have provoked him on his wife's death to have several of his love poems enclosed in her coffin. No matter what the fact of his poetry, it is by his painting quite than by his poems that Rossetti has a position as a enormous mystic, for despite his fondness for precise handling, most of his pictures are substantially of a mystical personality. They represent the scenes and incidents be said in dreams in a way comparable to the art of William Blake.

.

Paintings

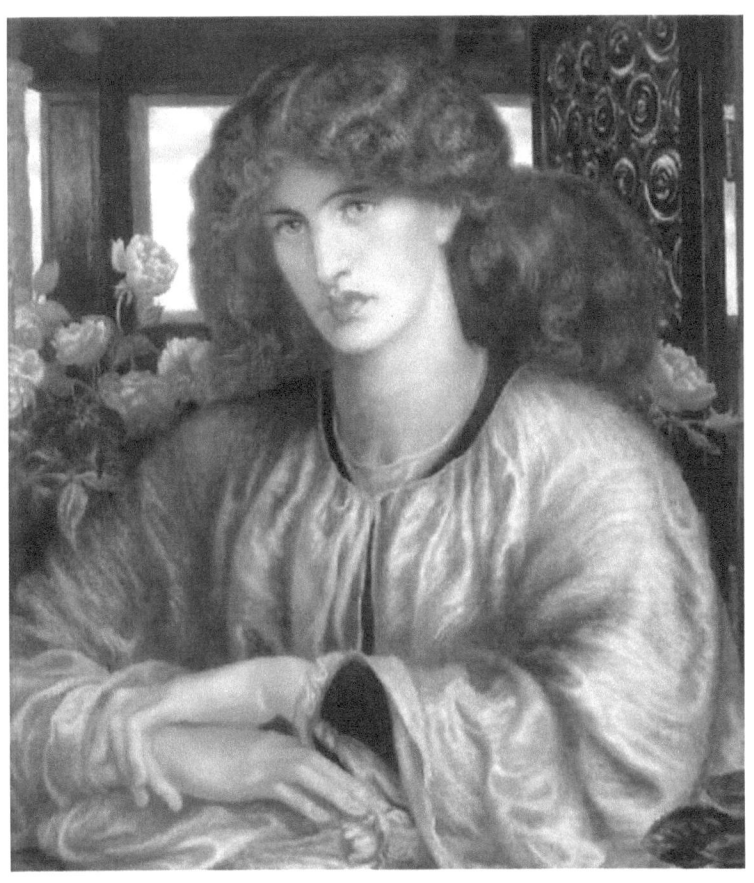

The lady at the window, 1879, oil on canvas

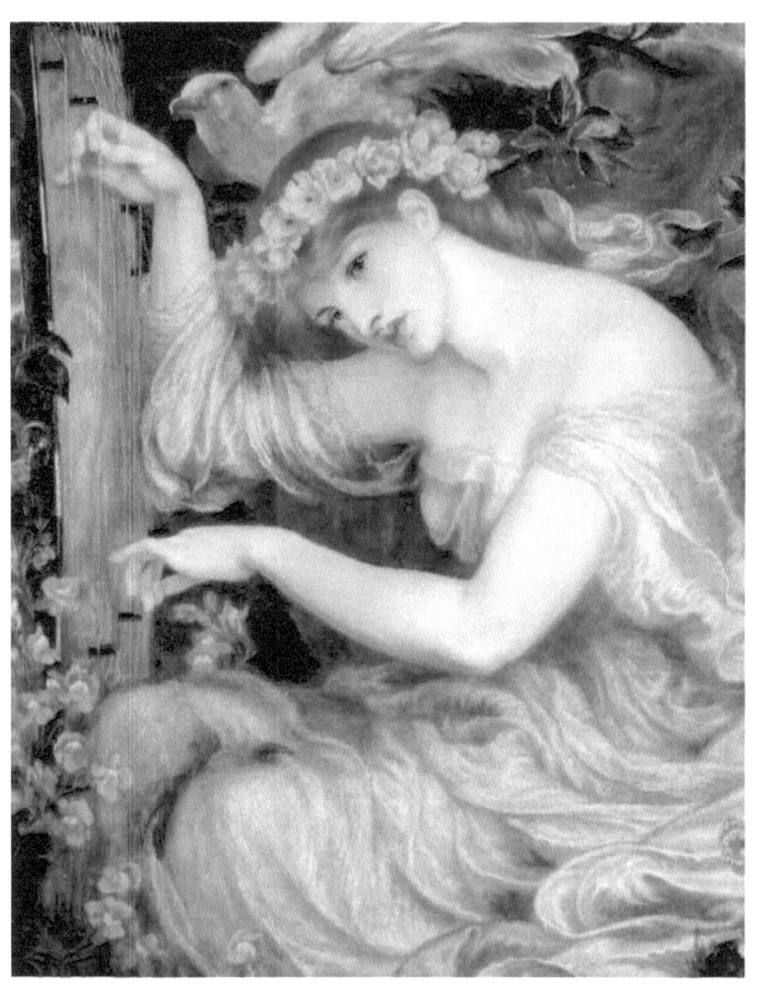

Sea period 1877, oil on canvas

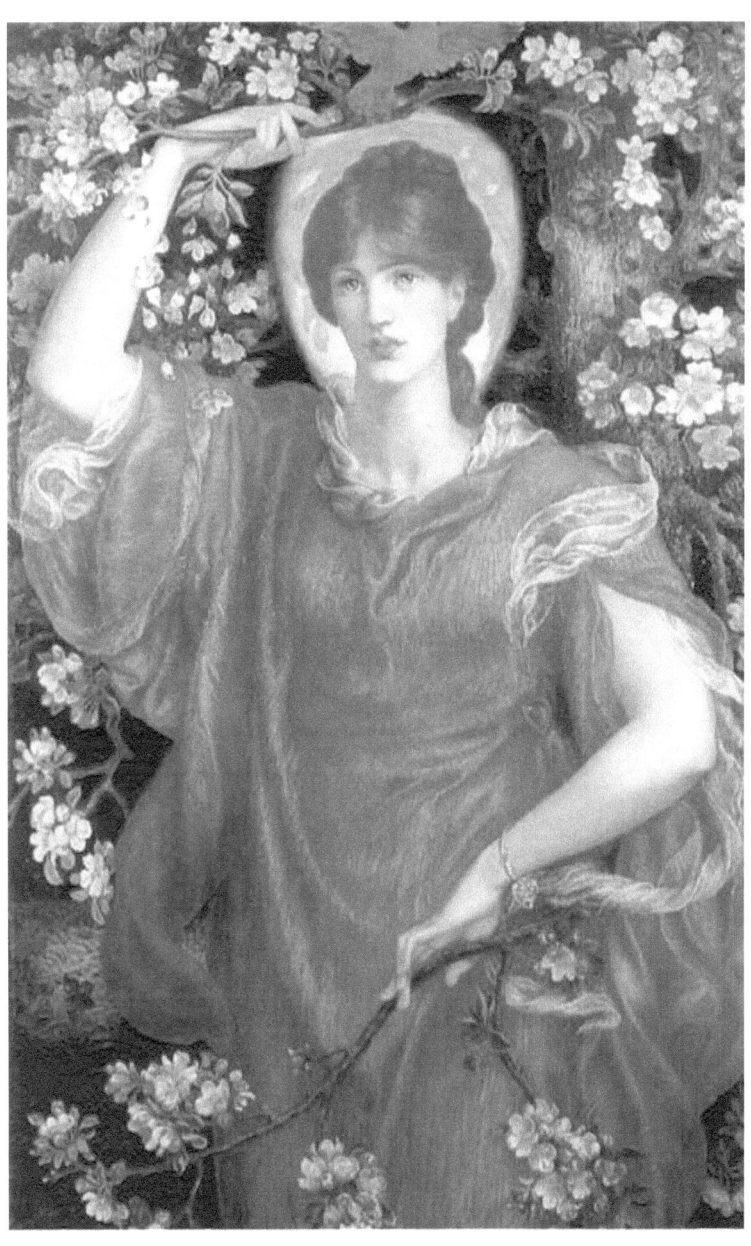

The vision of Fiammetta, 1878, oil on canvas

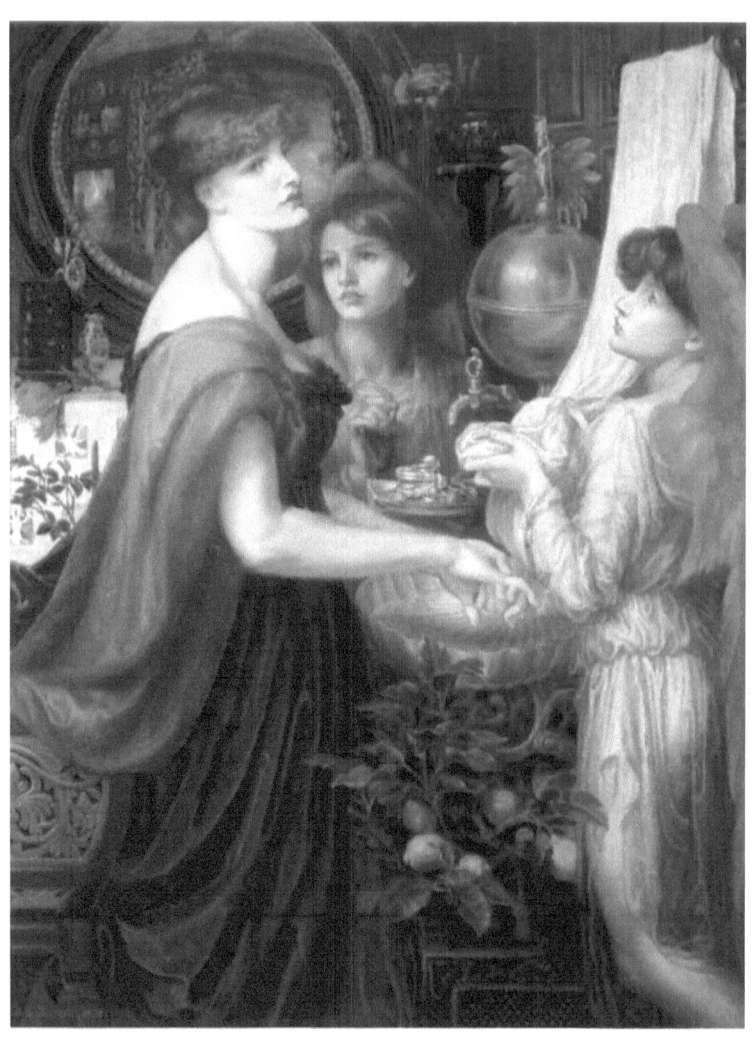

Beautiful hand (La Bella Mano), 1875, oil on canvas

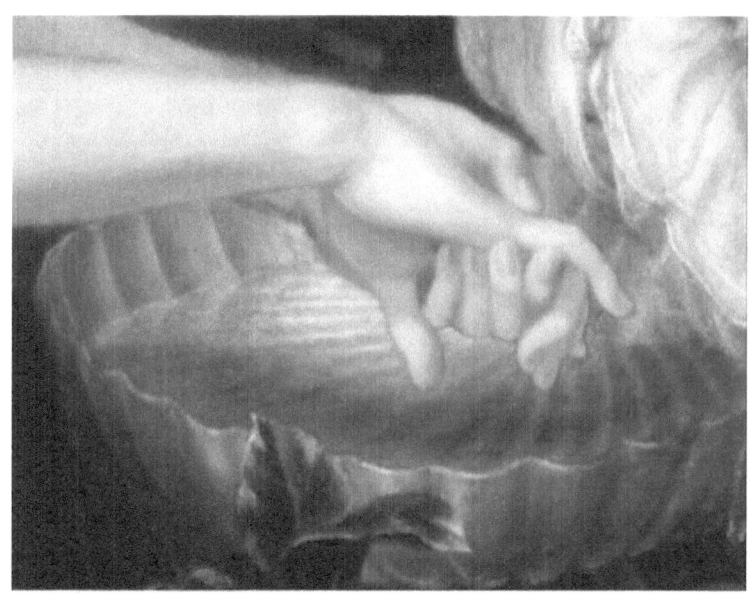

Beautiful hand (La Bella Mano), detail,1875, oil on canvas

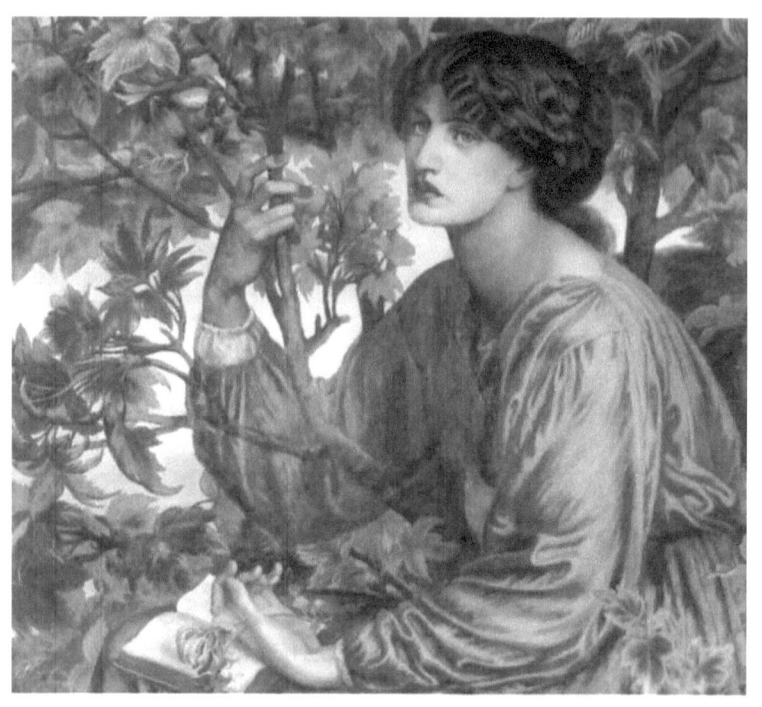

Day dream, 1880, oil on canvas

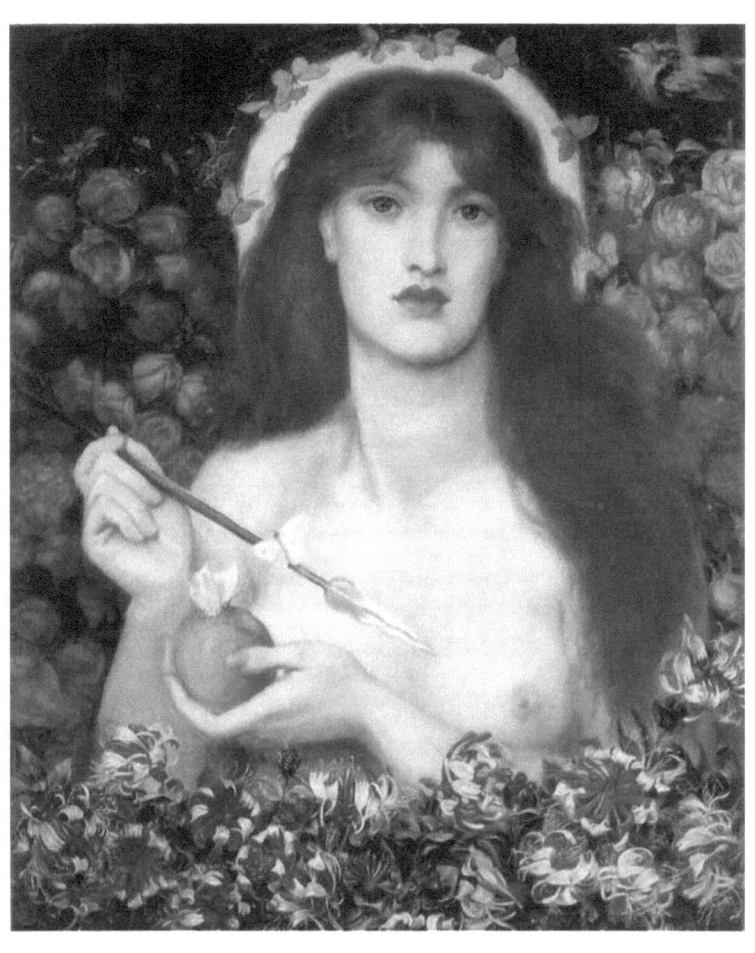

Venus Verticordia, 1881, oil on canvas

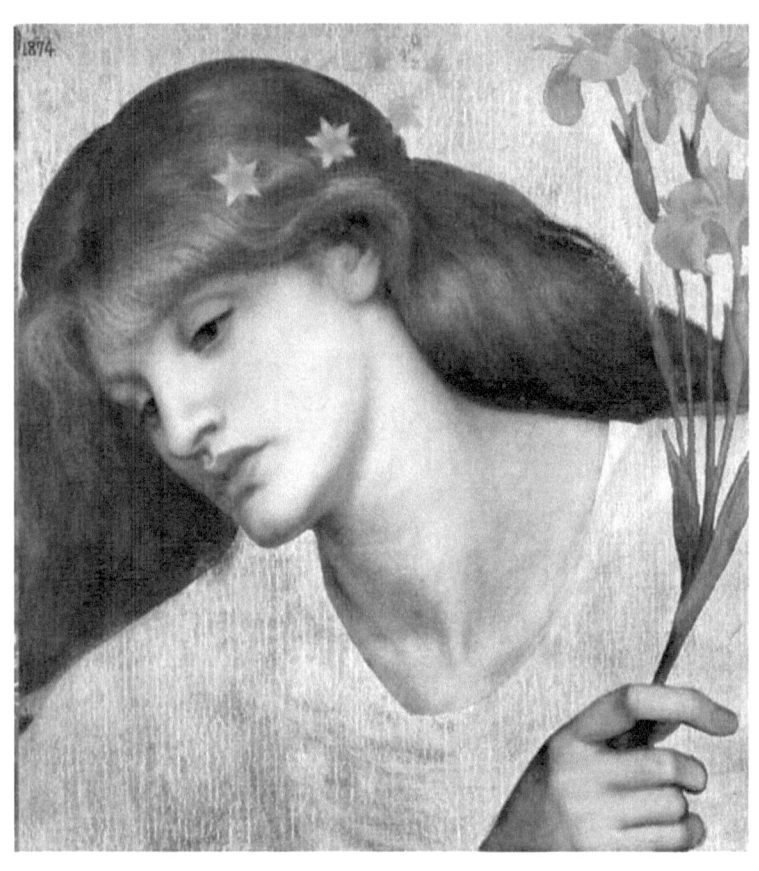

Sancta Lilias, 1875,oil on canvas

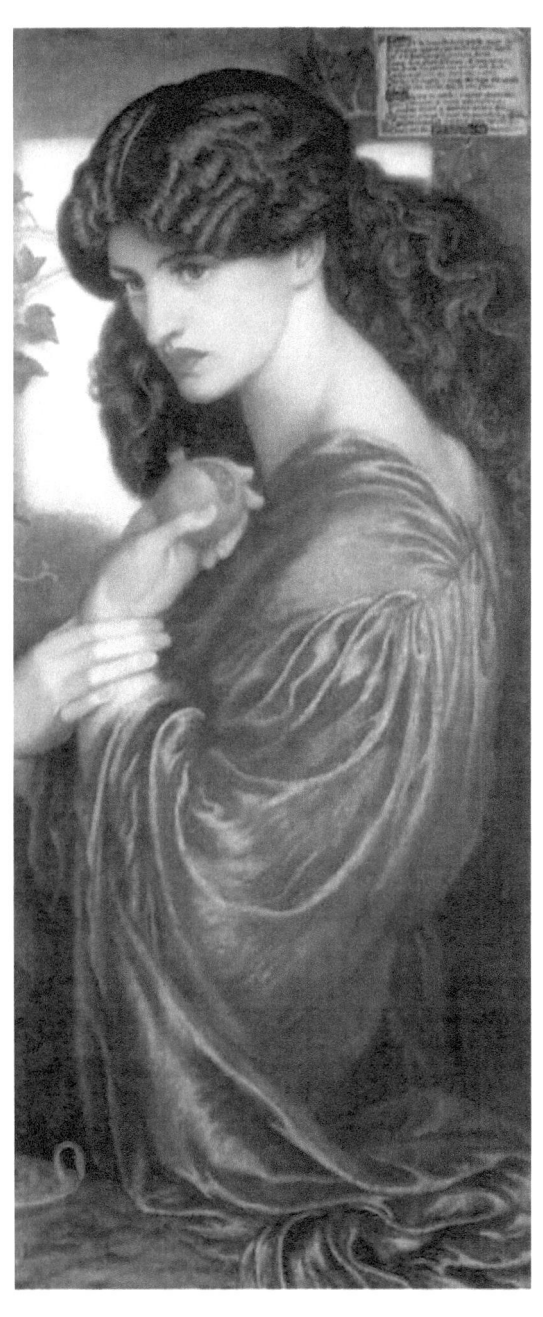

Proserpine, 1874, oil on canvas

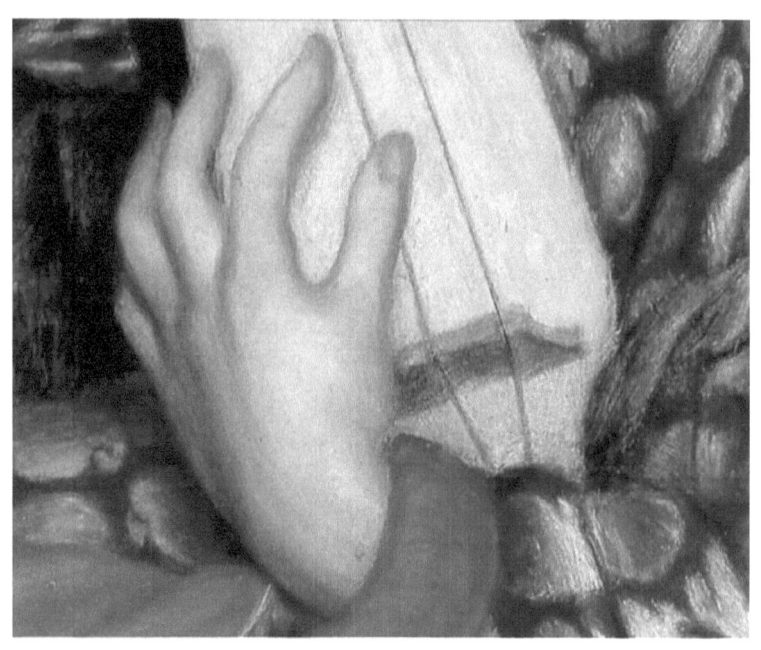

A Christmas Carol, detail, 1867, oil on canvas

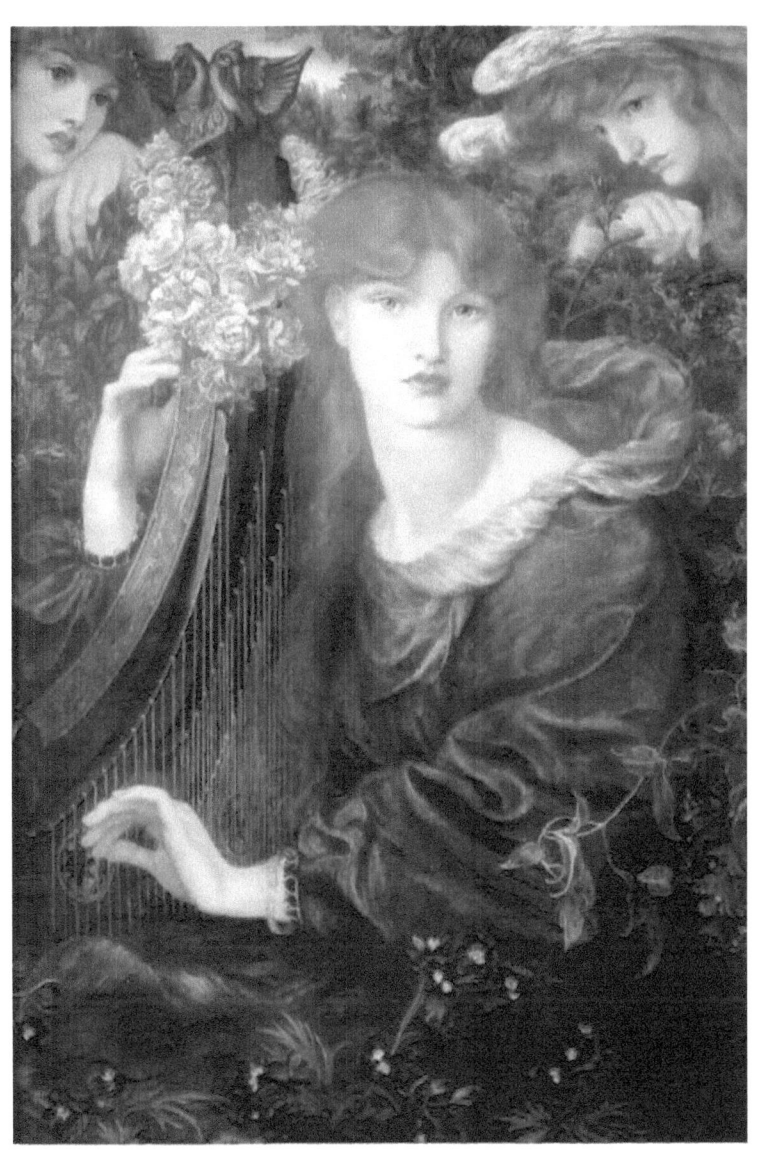

Monna Vanna, 1866, oil on canvas

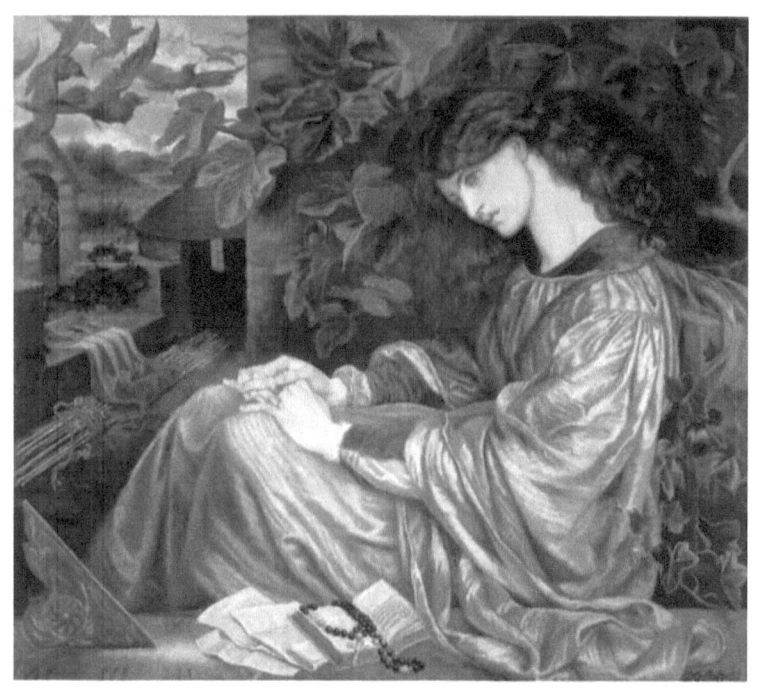

La Pia de Tolommei,1868, oil on canvas

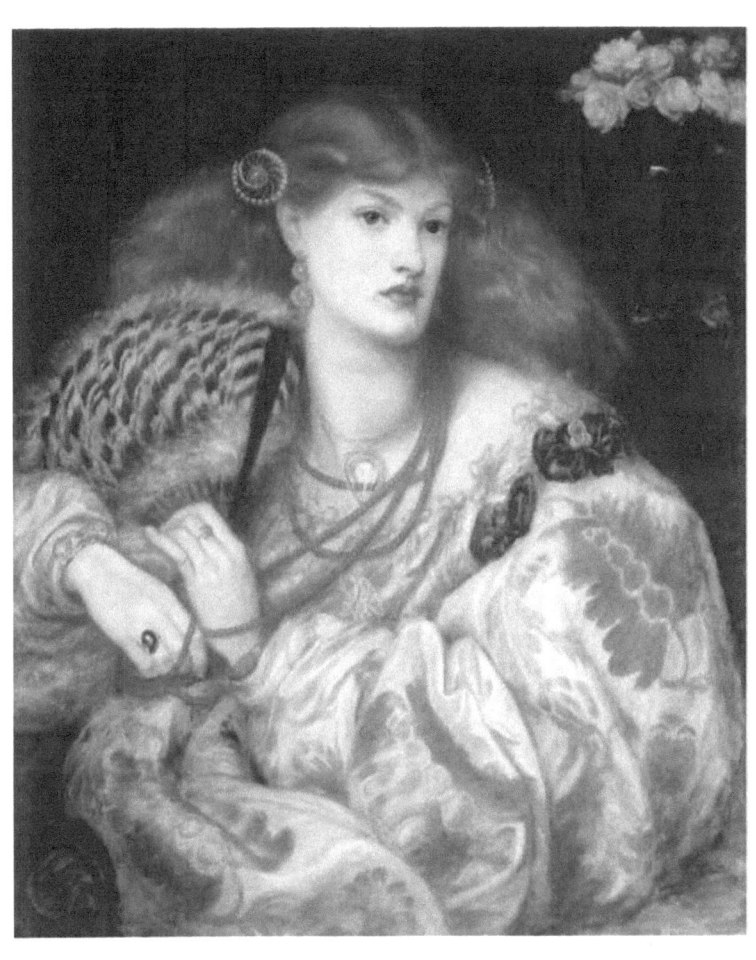

Monna Vanna, 1866, oil on canvas

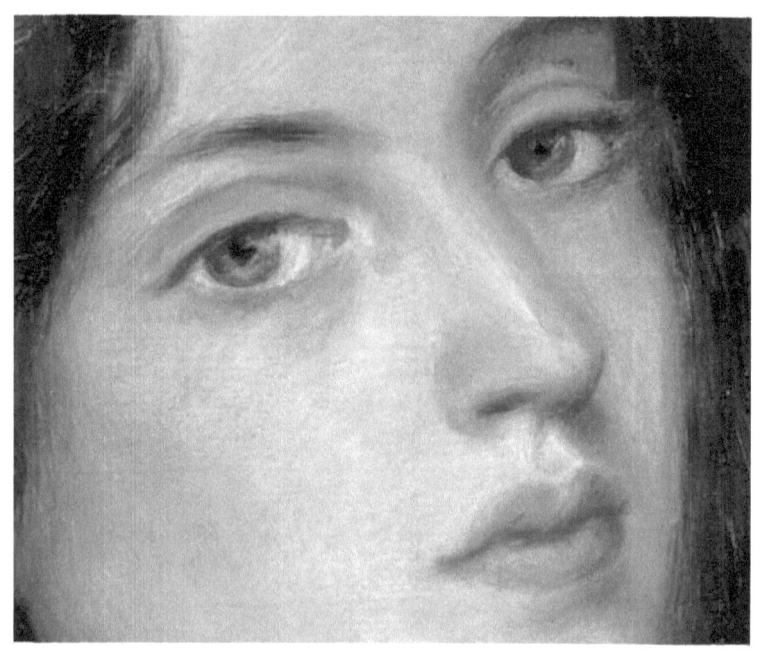

Miss Burton (detail), 1869, oil on canvas

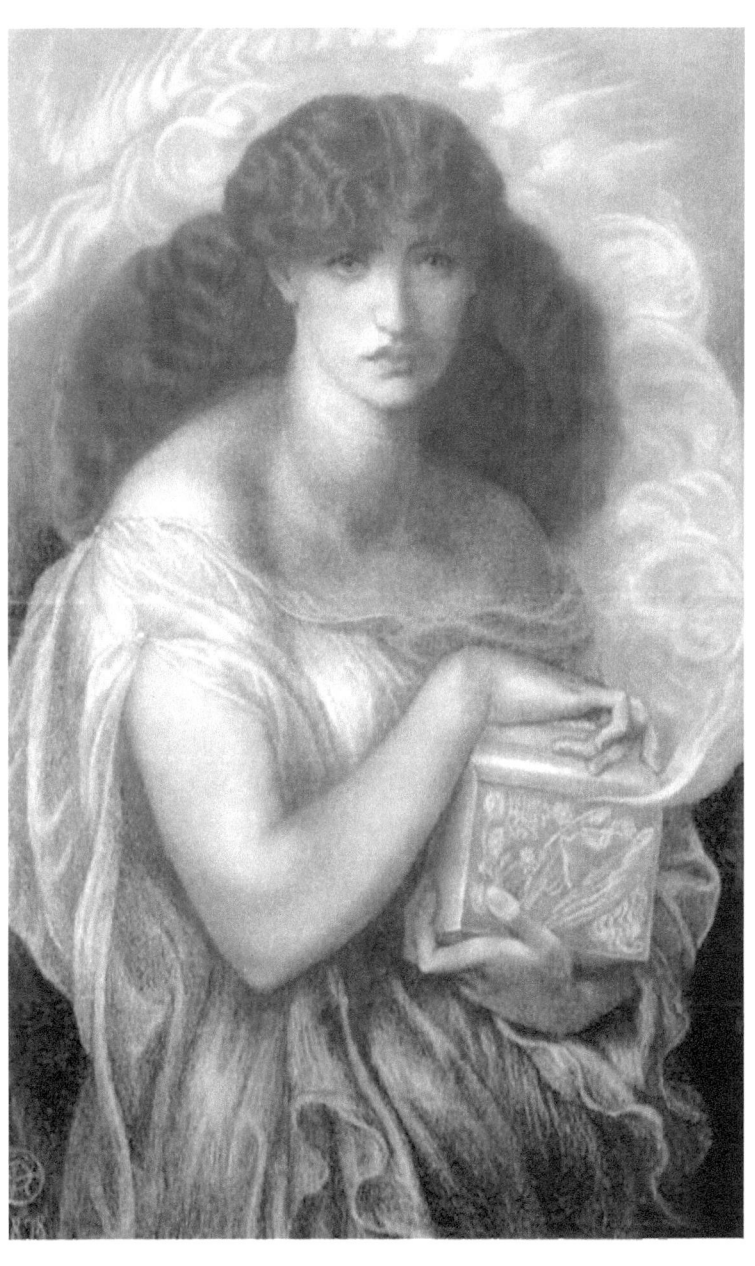

Pandora, 1870, oil on canvas

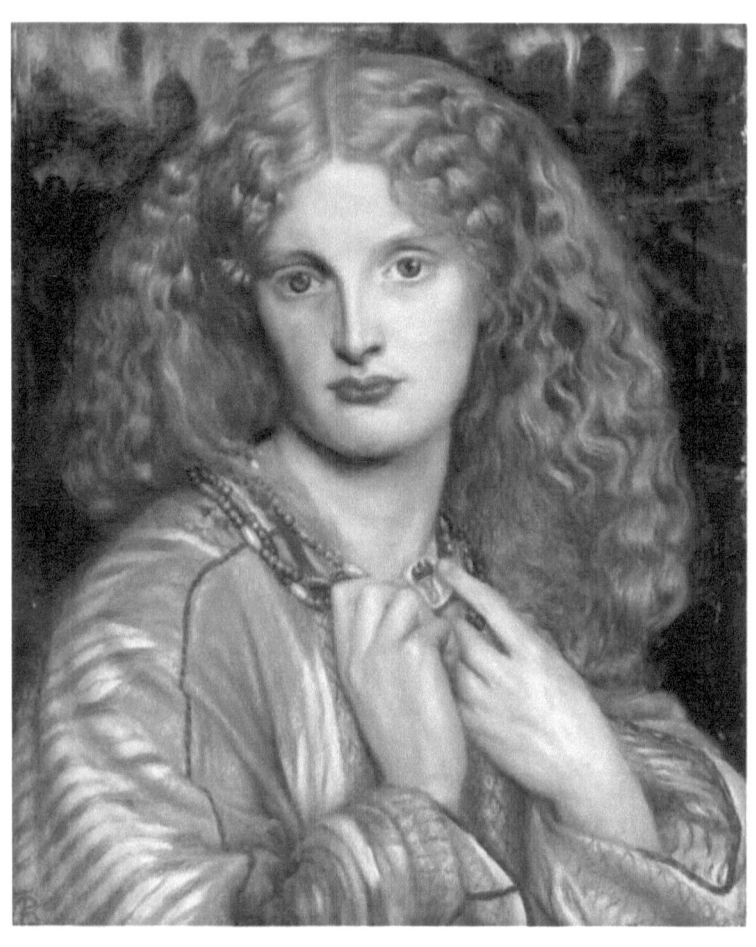

Beautiful Helen, 1863, oil on canvas

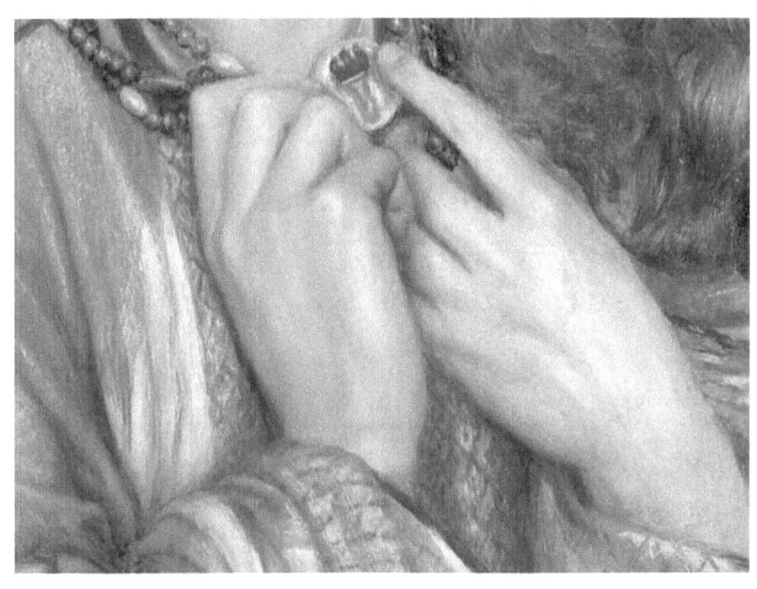

Beautiful Helen, 1863, detail,oil on canvas

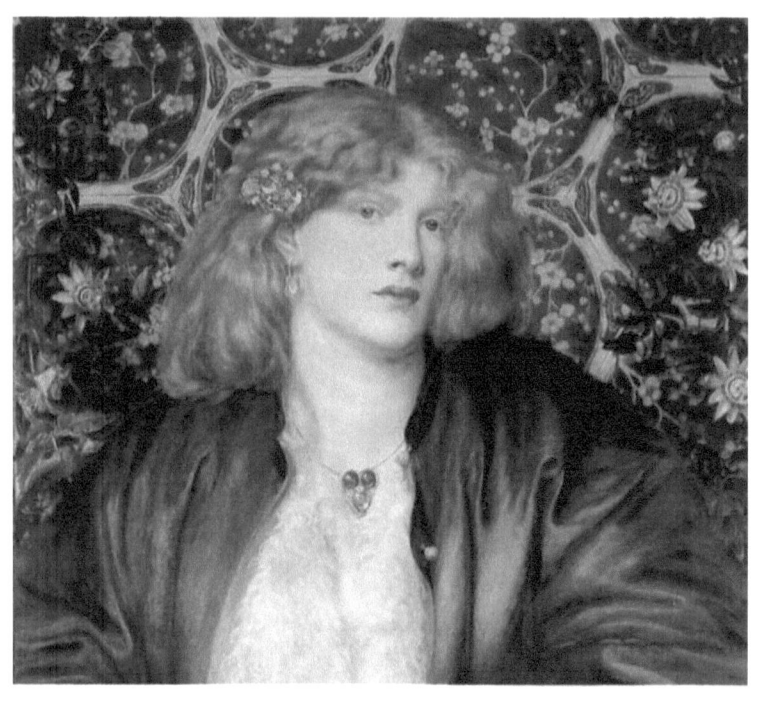

Blue Boudoir, 1869, oil on canvas

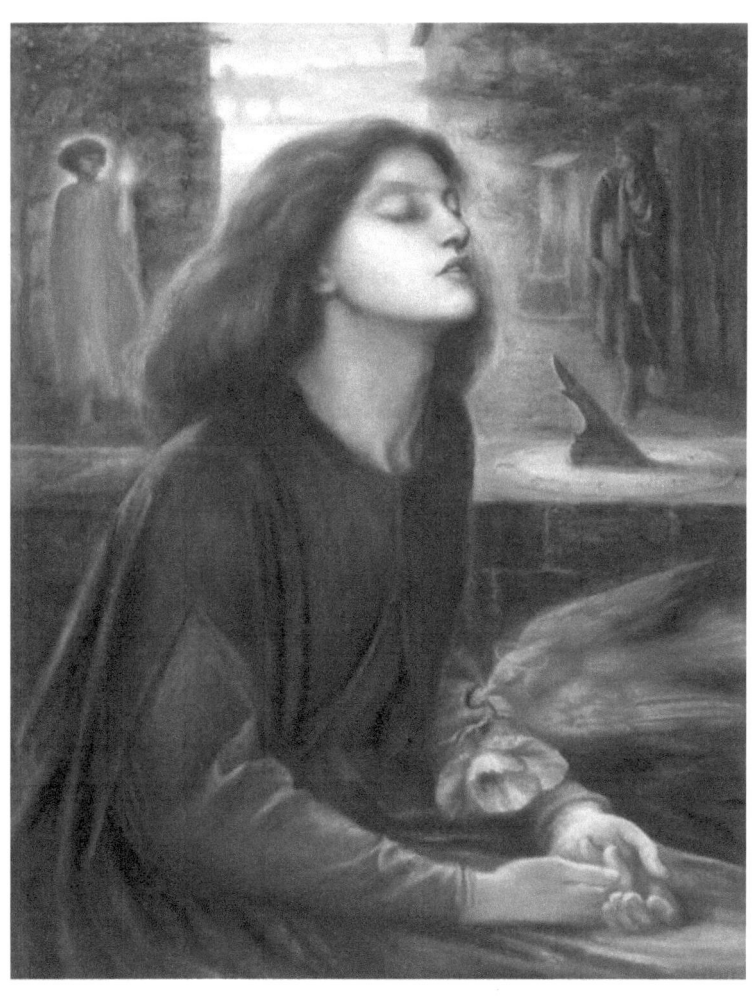

Blessed Beatrice, 1870, oil on canvas

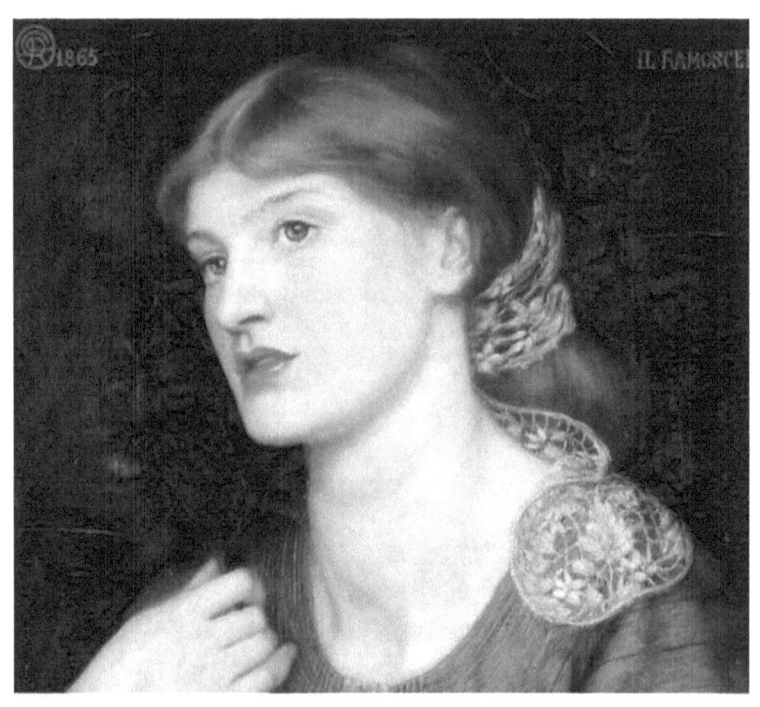

Il Ramoscello, 1865, oil on canvas

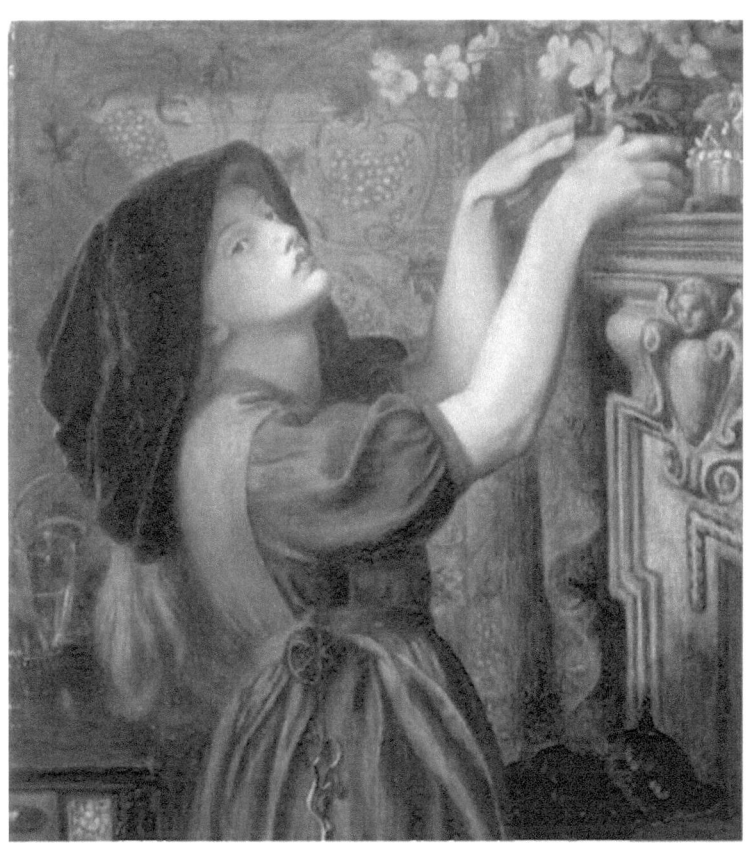

Gardener's Daughter, 1873, oil on canvas

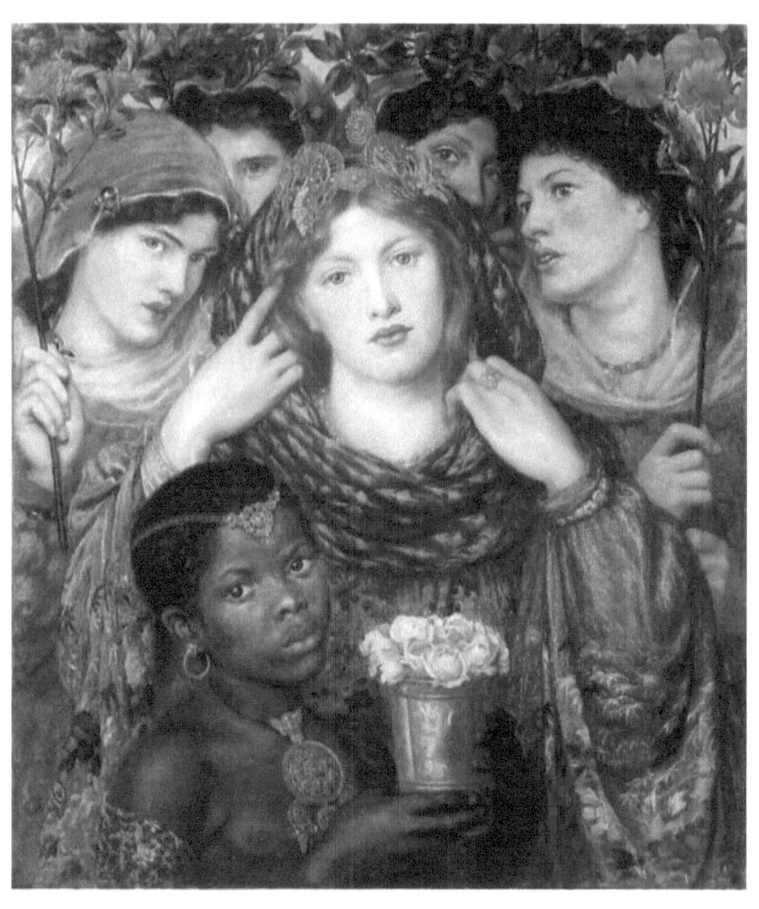

Bride, 1876, oil on canvas

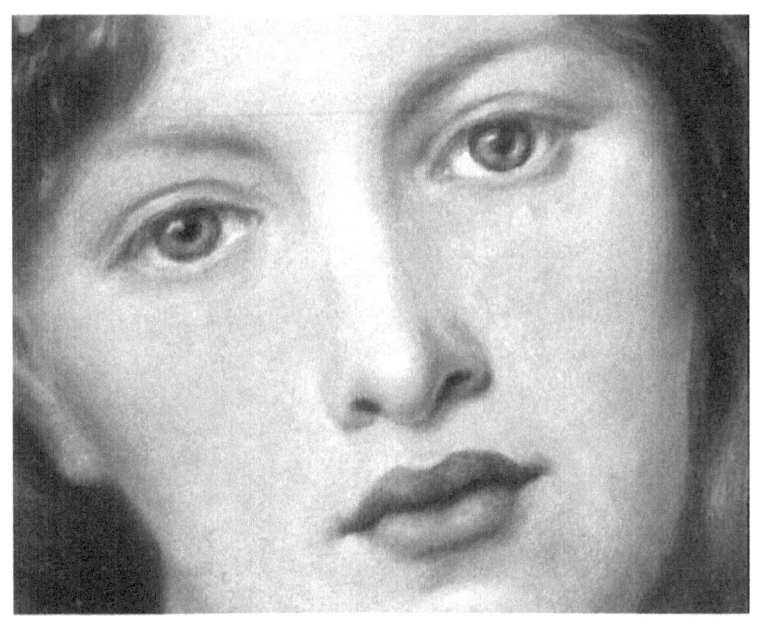

Bride, detail, 1876, oil on canvas

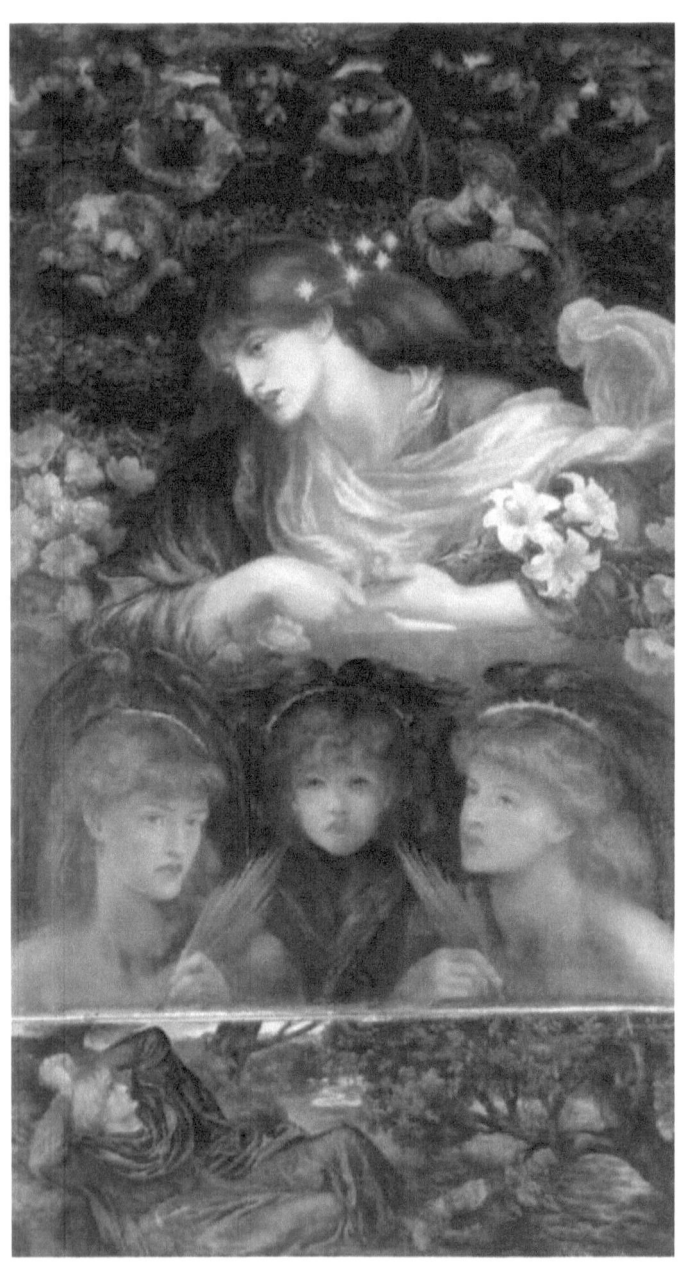

Blessed Damozel, 1878, oil on canvas

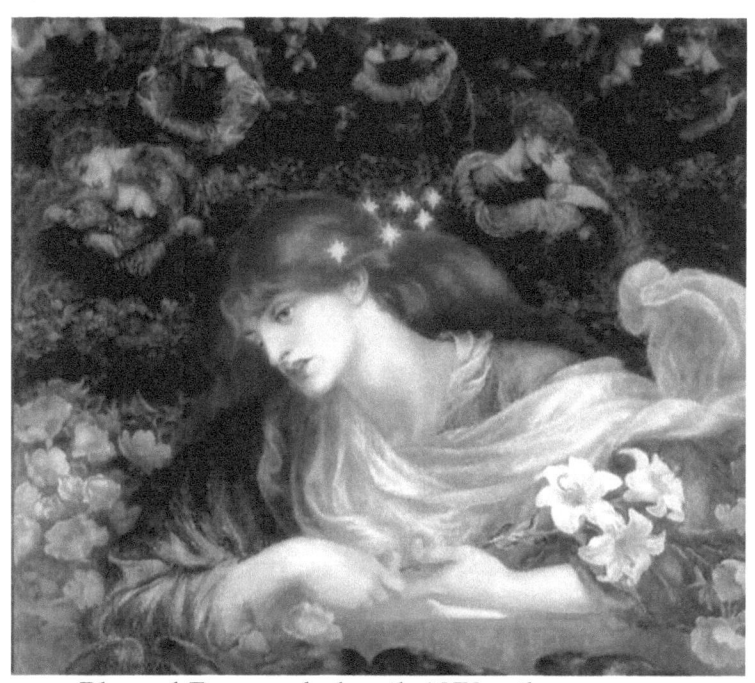

Blessed Damozel, detail, 1878, oil on canvas

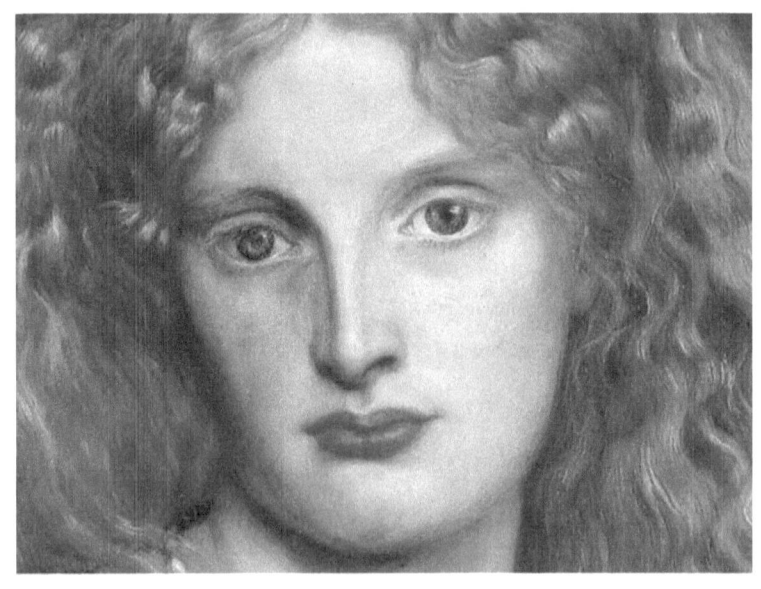

Beautiful Helen (detail), oil on canvas

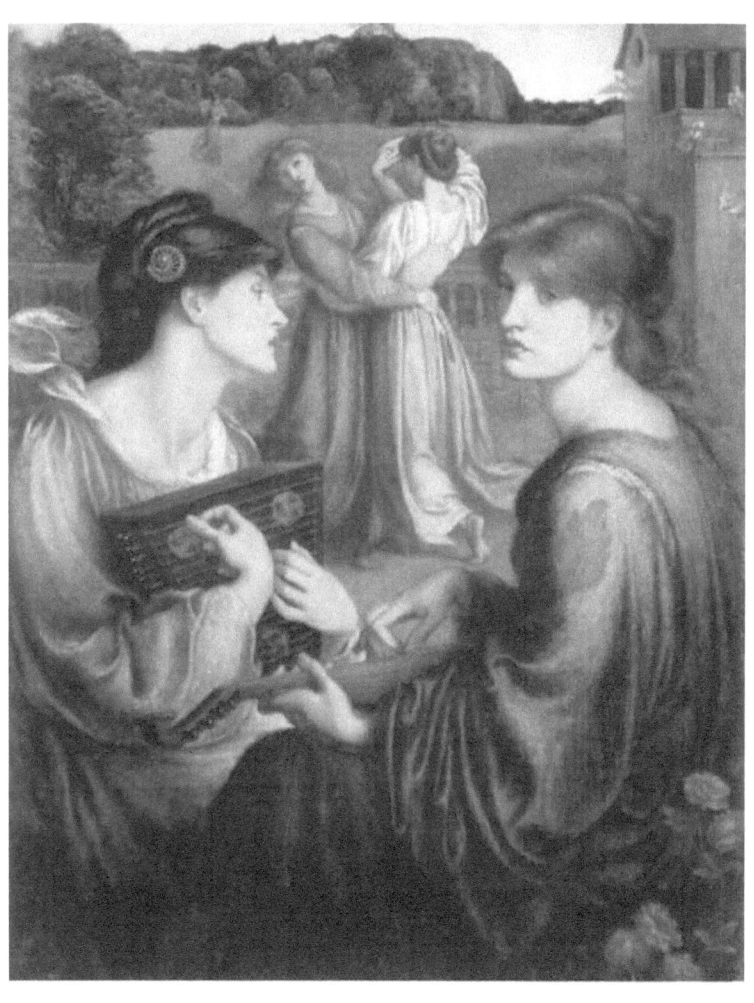

Pavilion in the meadow, 1872, oil on canvas

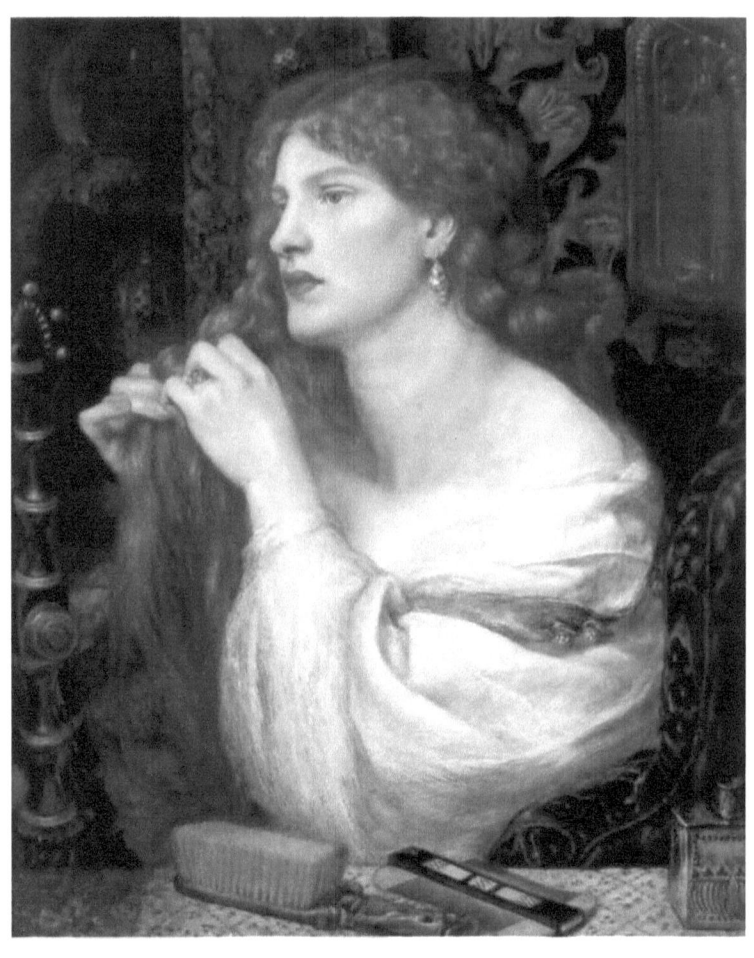

Fazio's Mistress, 1863, oil on canvas

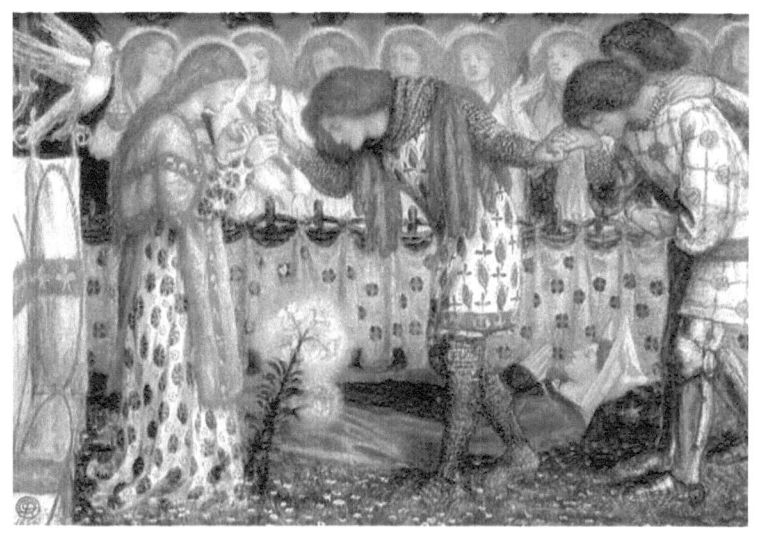

Sir Galahad, 1859, mixed media with watercolor on paper

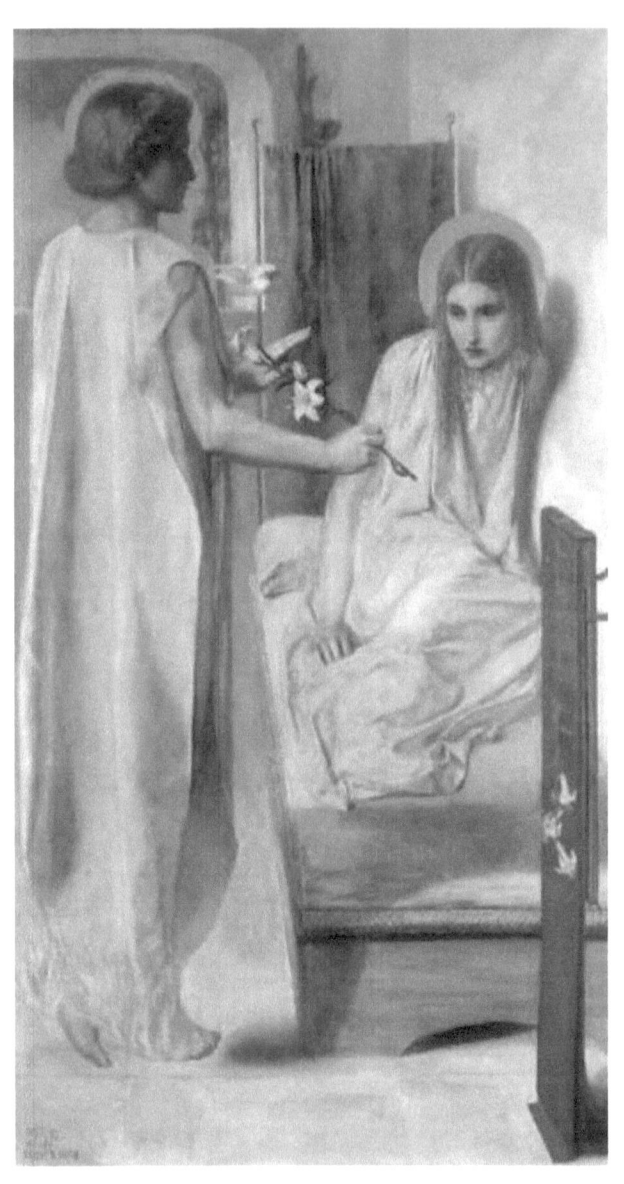

Annunciation, 1850, oil on canvas

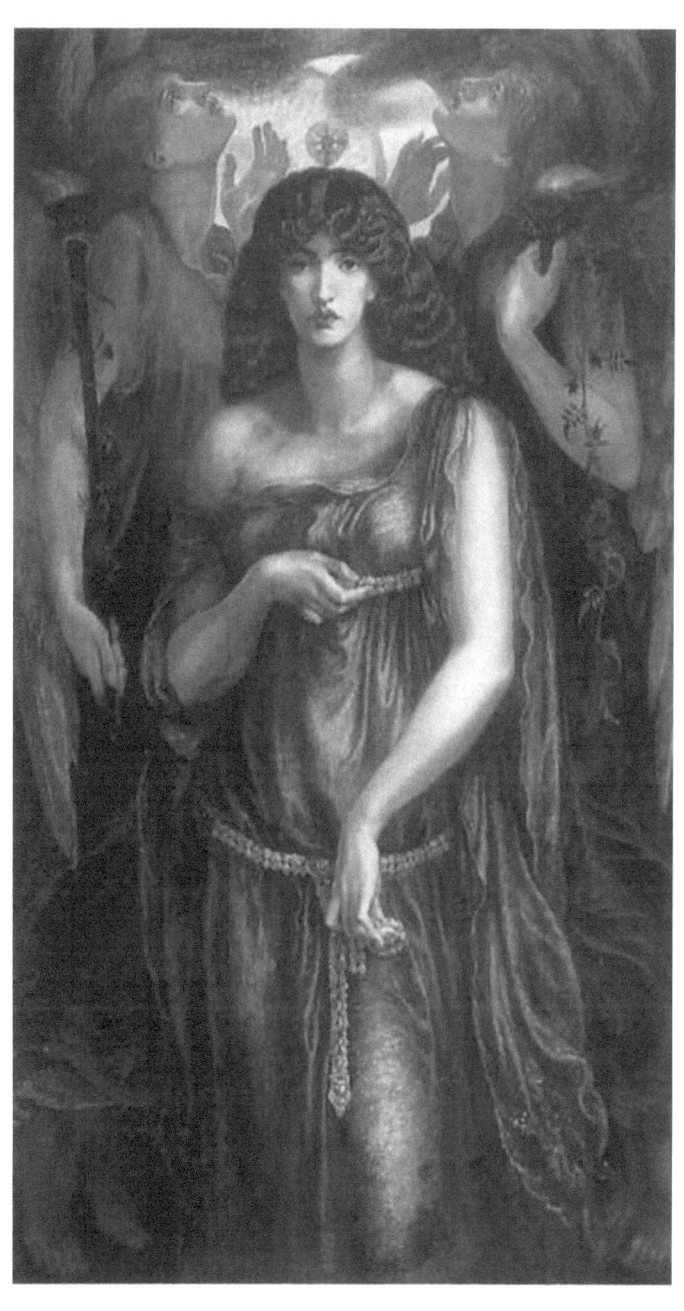

Astarte Syriaca, 1877, oil on canvas

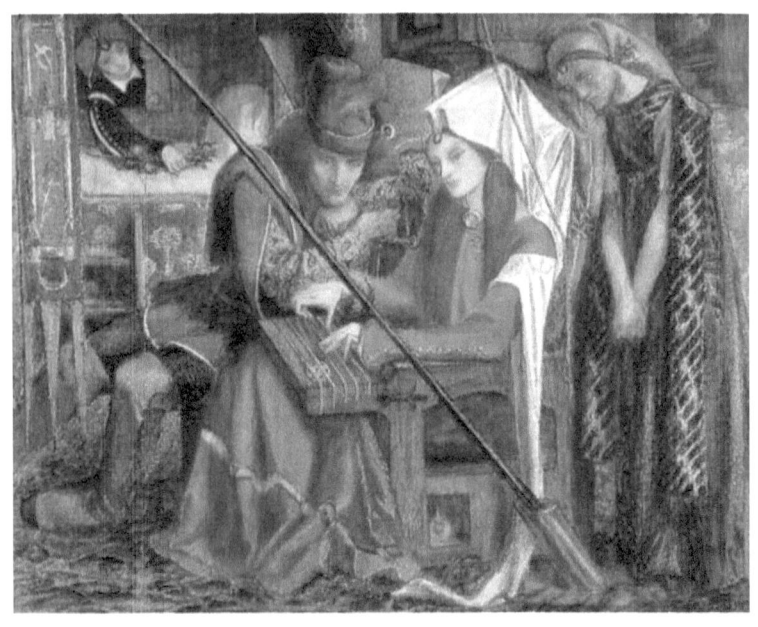

Melody of the Seven Towers, 1857, watercolor on paper

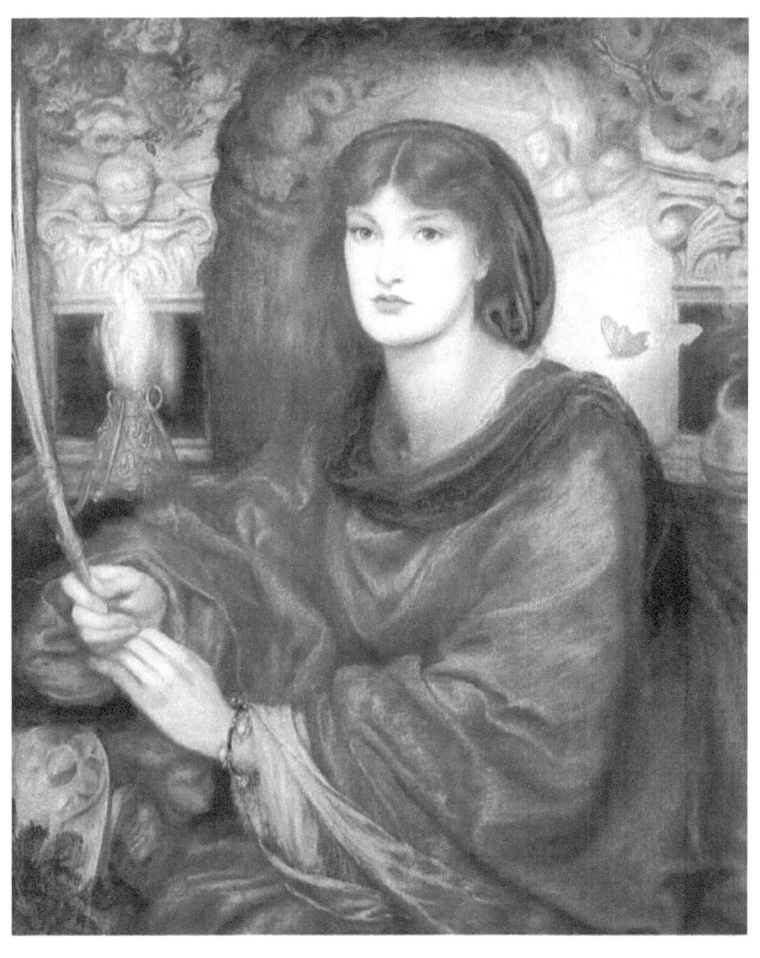

Sybila Palmifella, 1876, oil on canvas

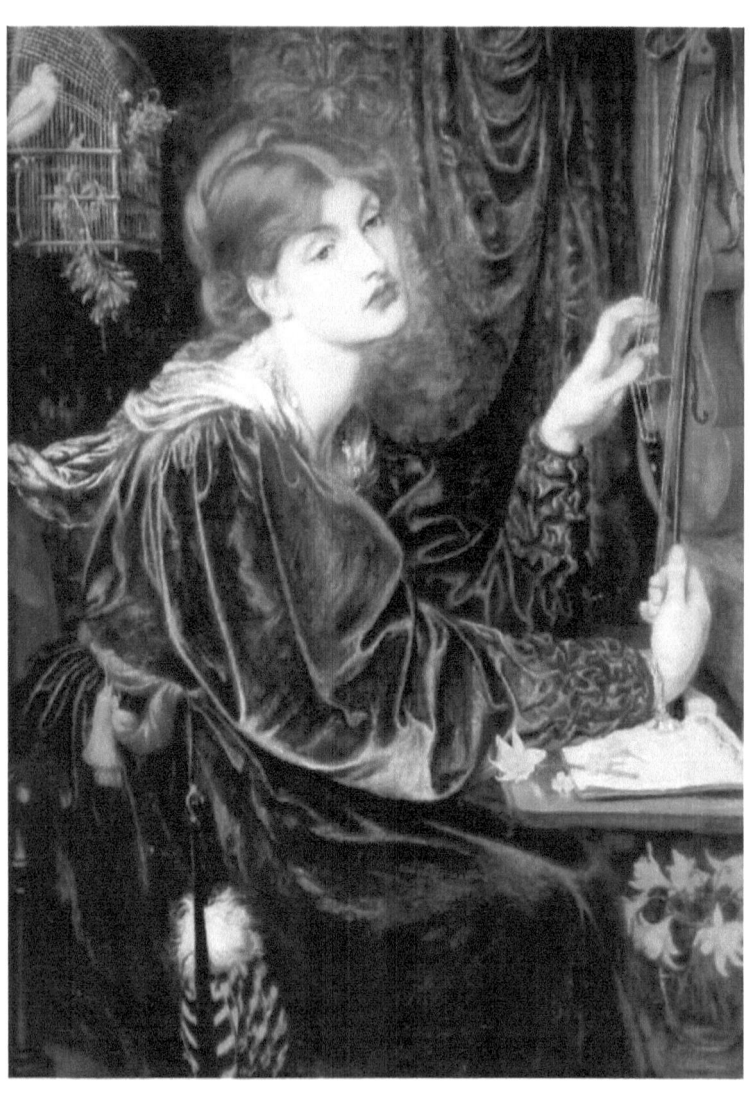

Veronica Veronese, 1872, oil on canvas

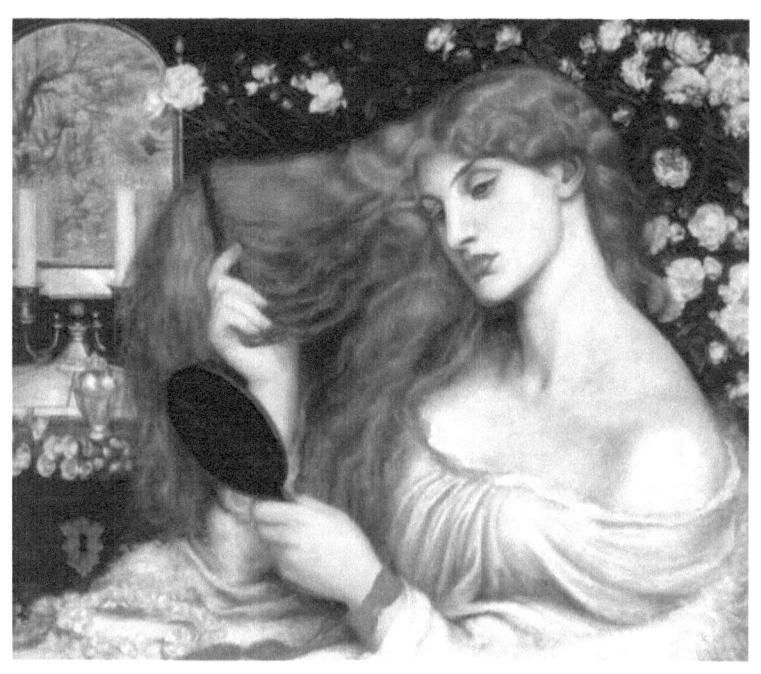

Lady Lilith, 1868, oil on canvas

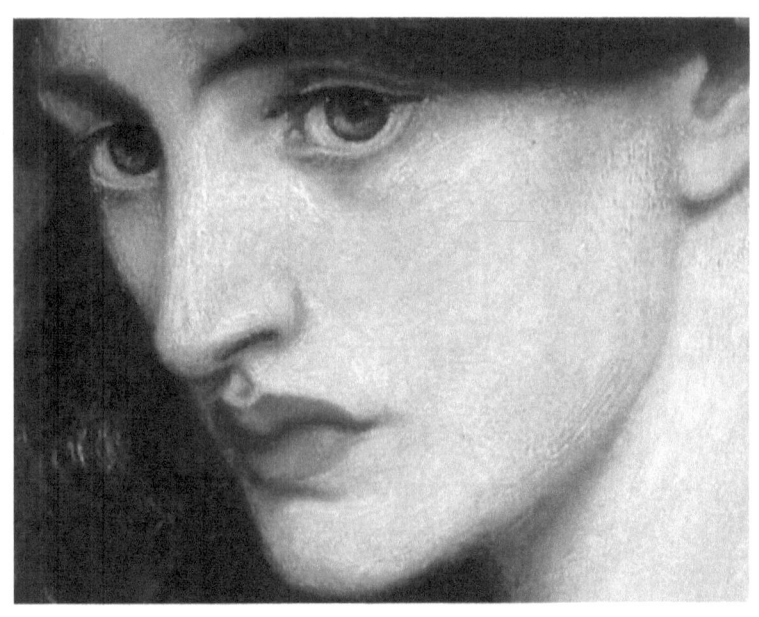

Snowdrops (detail), 1873, oil on canvas

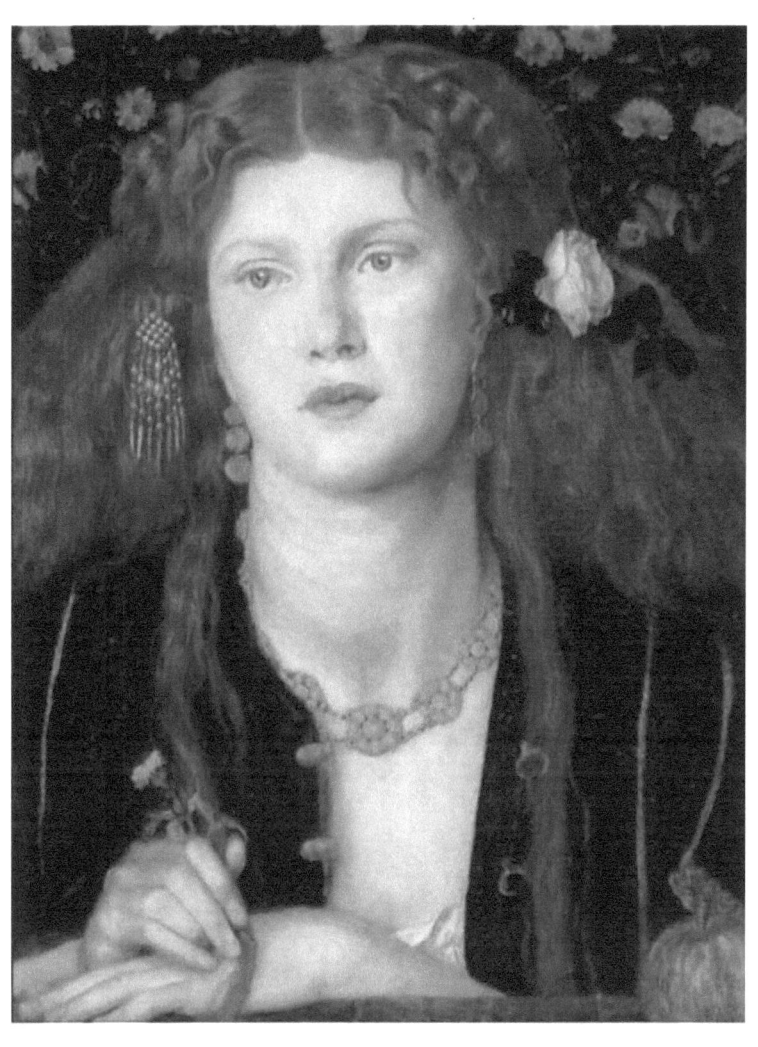

Kissed lips, 1859, oil on wood

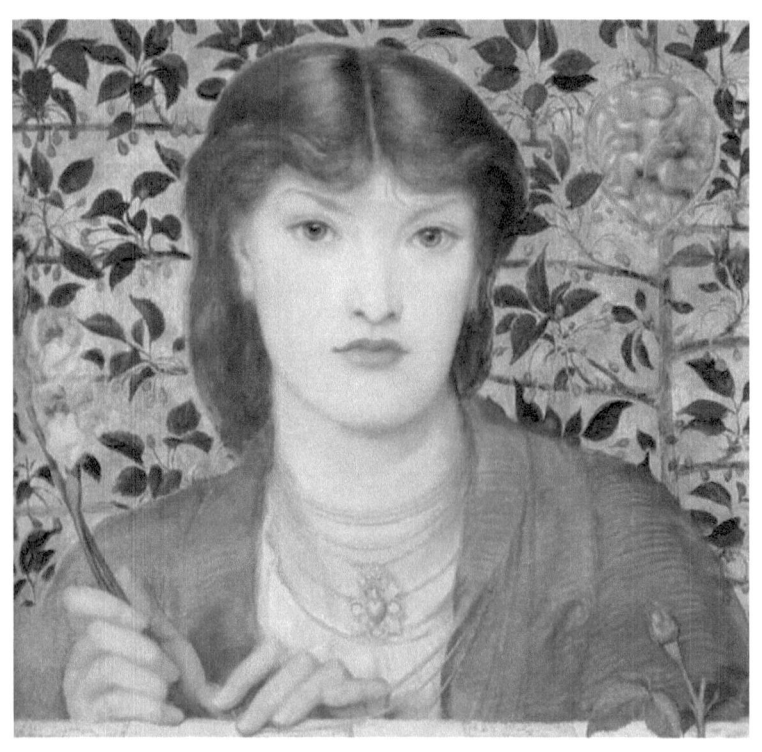

Beloved, 1866, oil on canvas

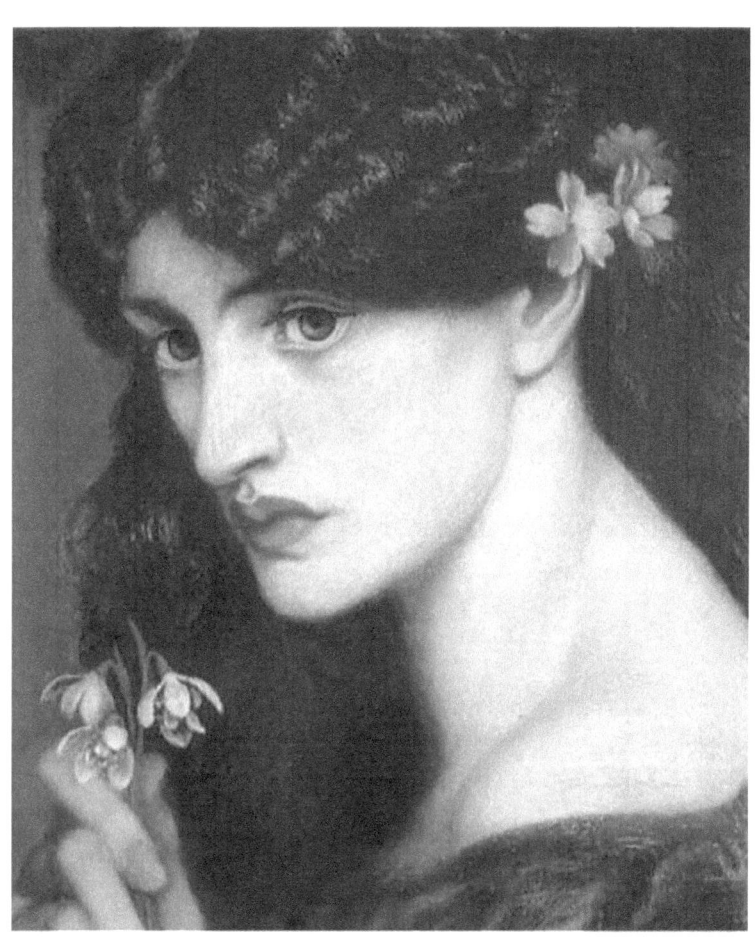

Snowdrops, 1873, oil on canvas

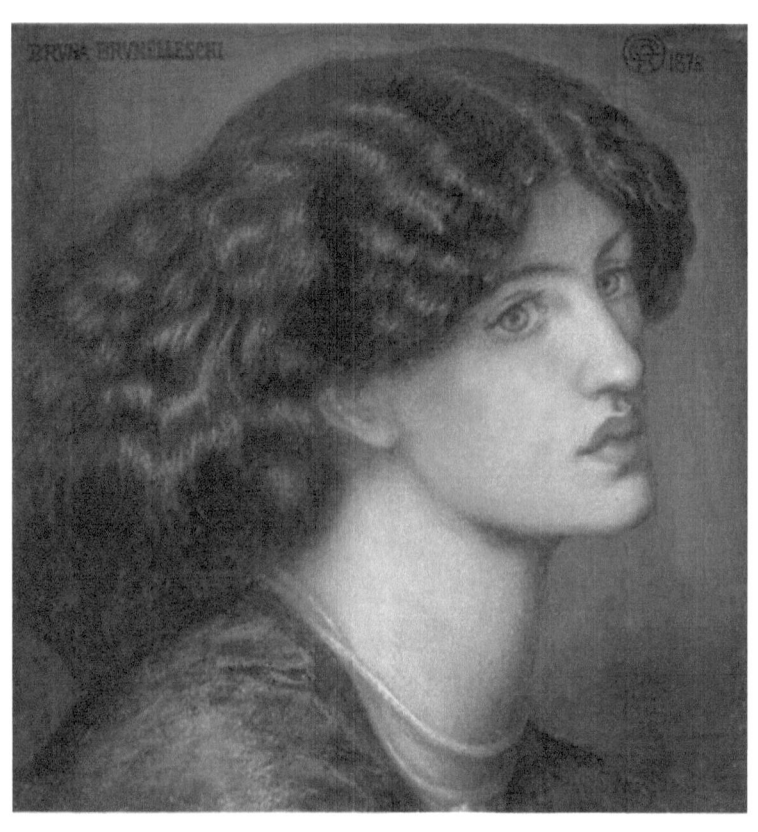

Bruna Brunelelleschi, 1878, watercolor on paper

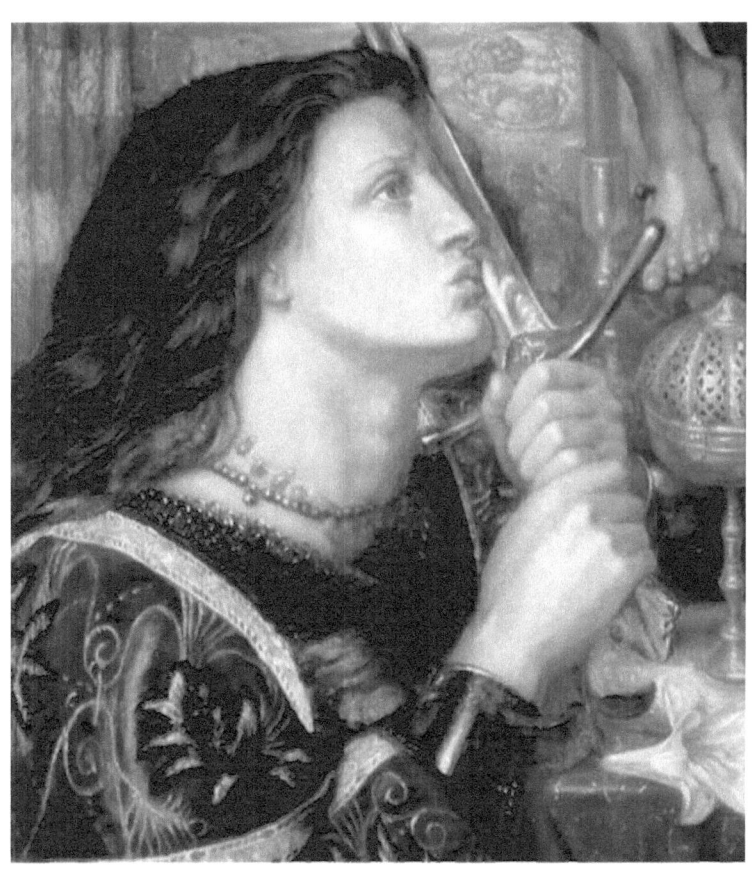

Joan of Arc kissing the Sword of Liberation(detail),
1863, oil on canvas

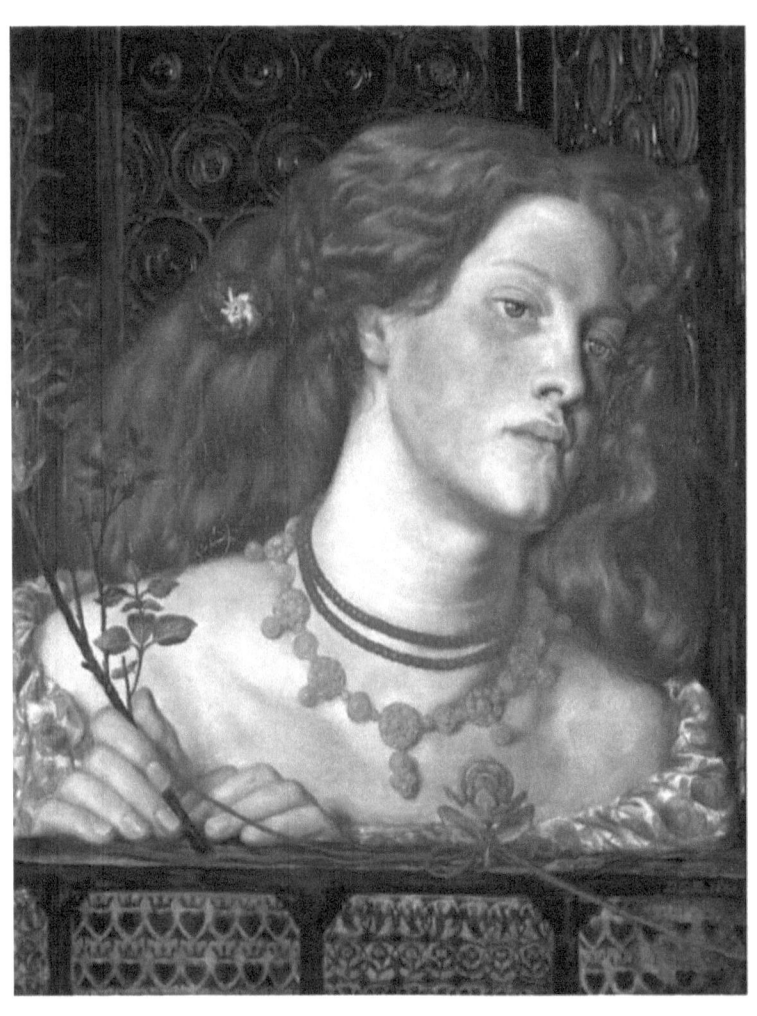

Fair Rosamund, 1861, oil on canvas

Drawings

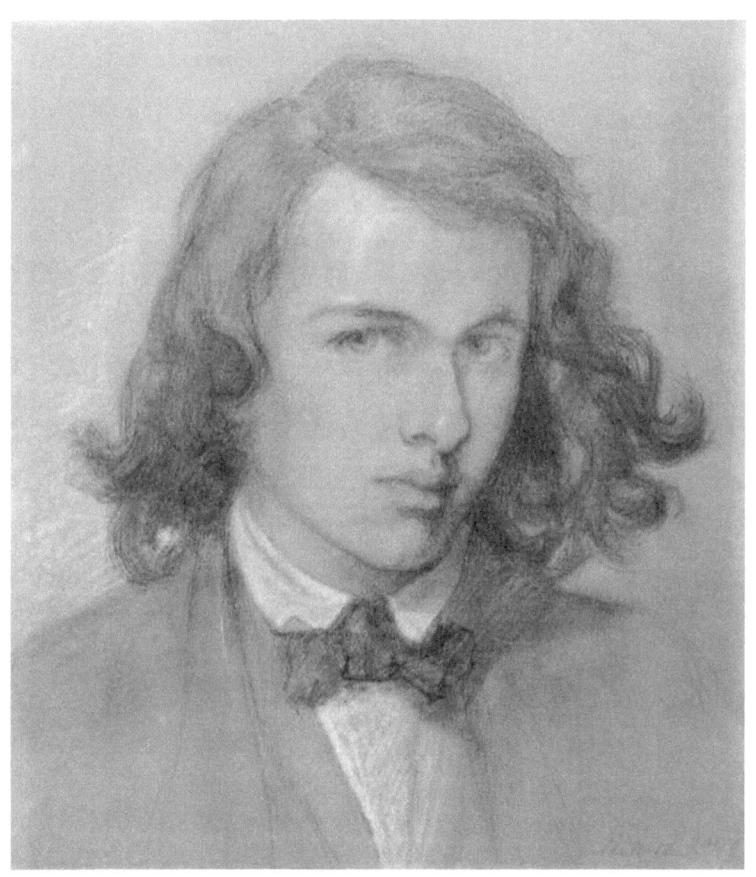

Self-portrait, 1847

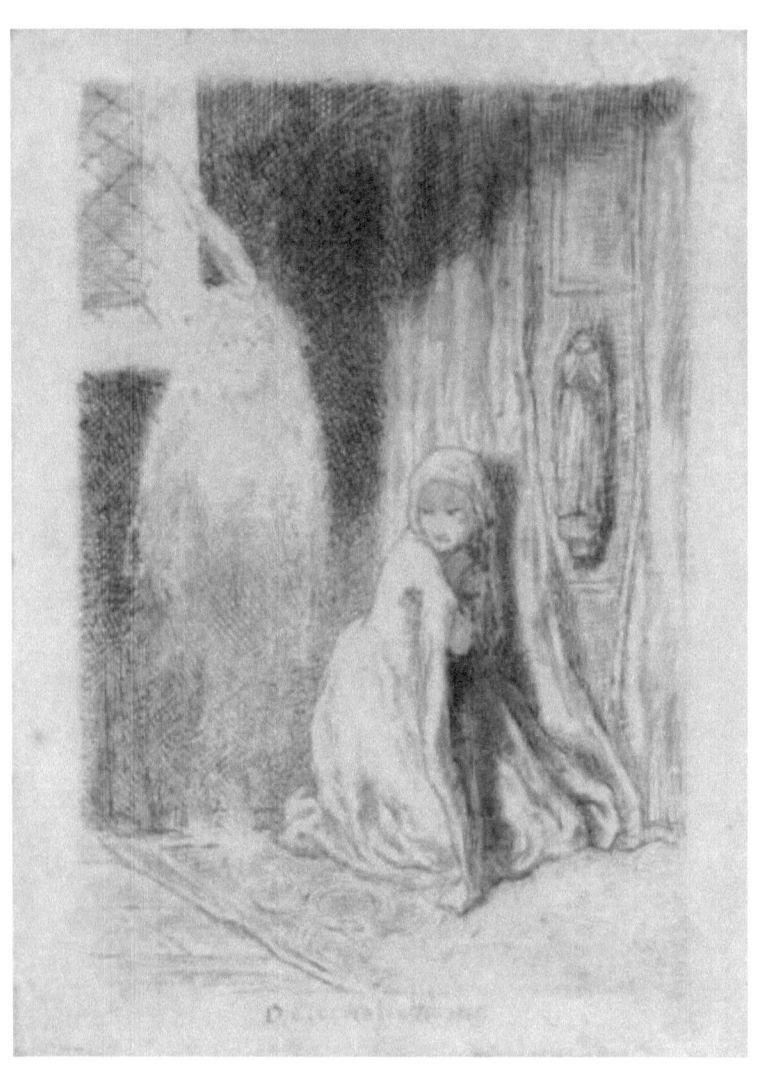

Faust: Margaret in the Church, 1848

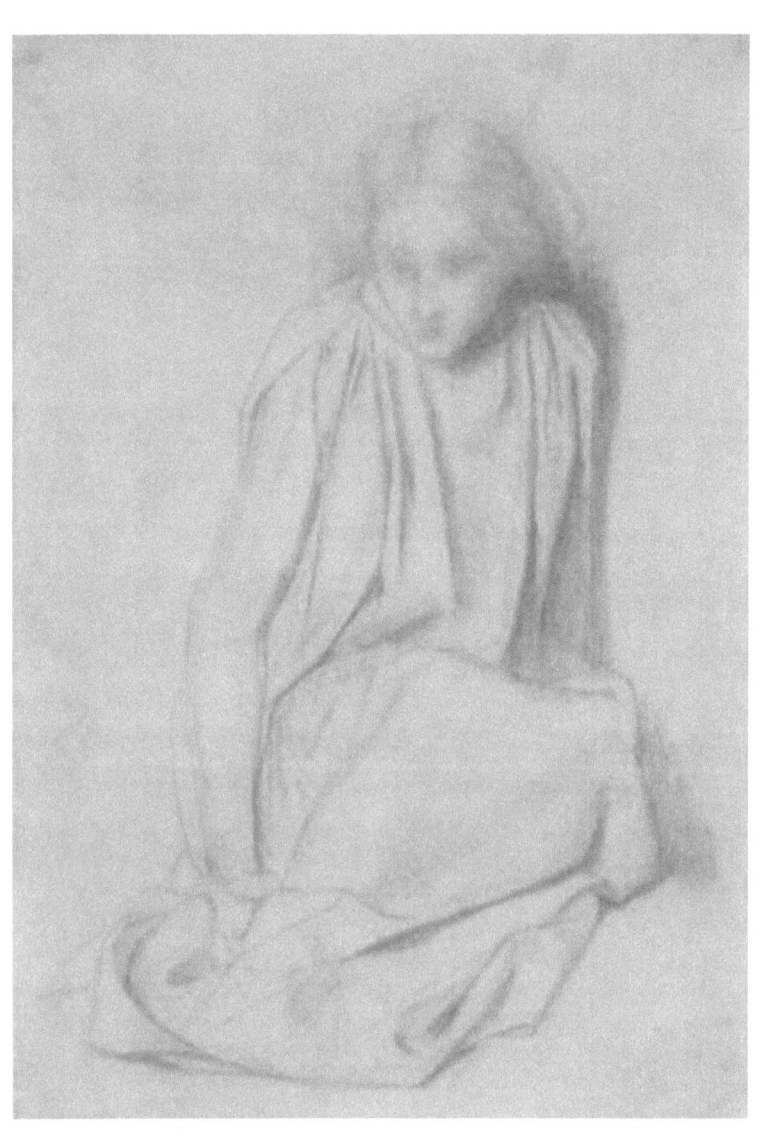

Ecce Ancilla Domini!, circa 1849

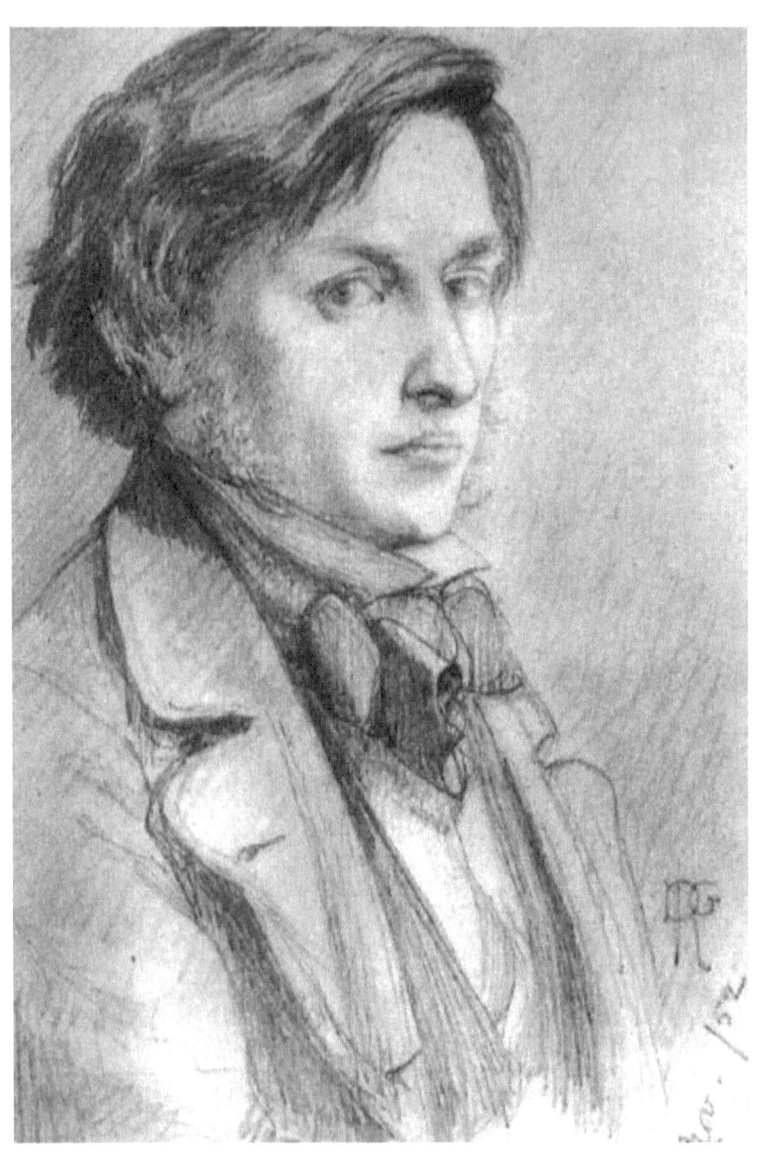

Portrait of Ford Madox Brown, circa 1852

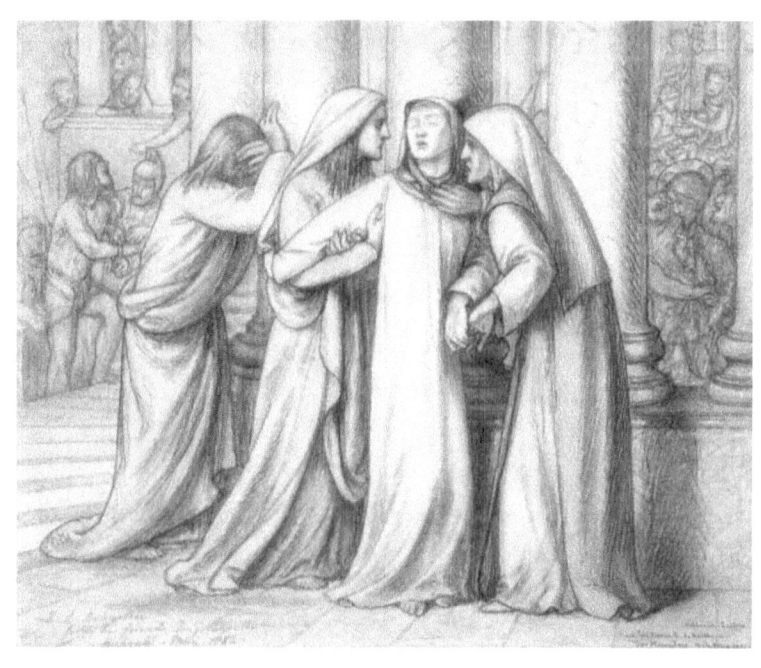

The Virgin Mary Being Comforted, 1852

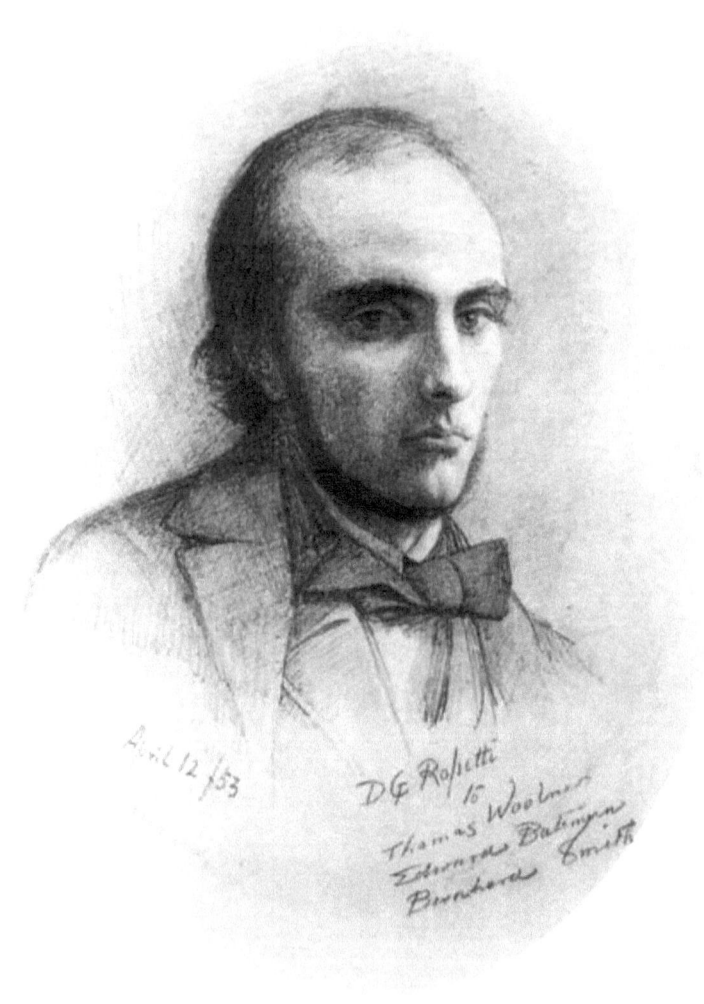

Portrait of William Rossetti, 1853

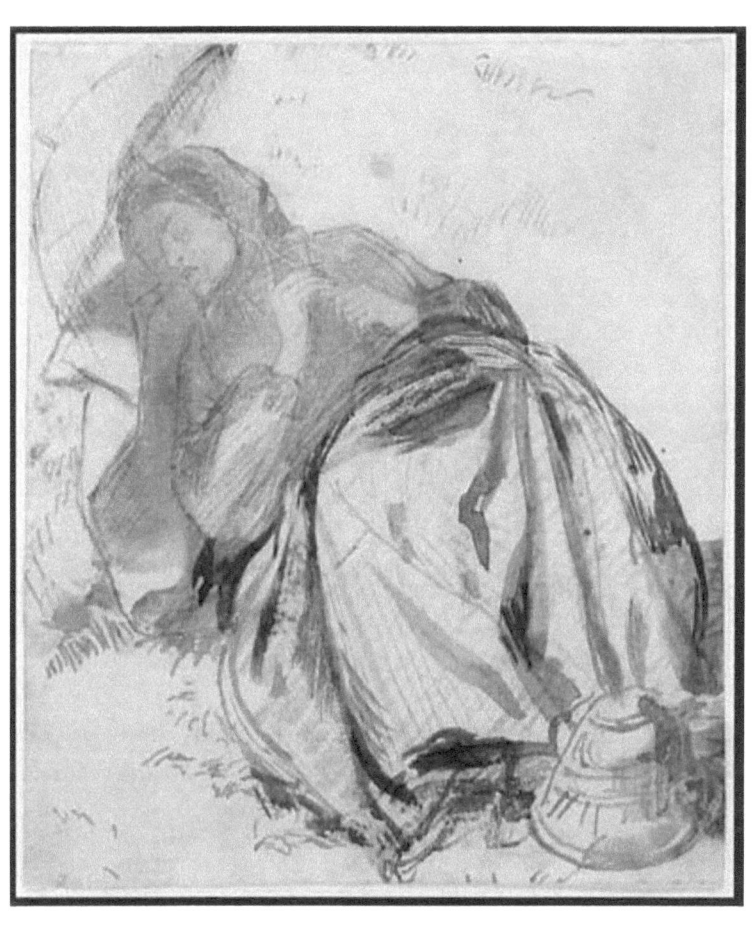

Elizabeth Siddal, 1852-1855

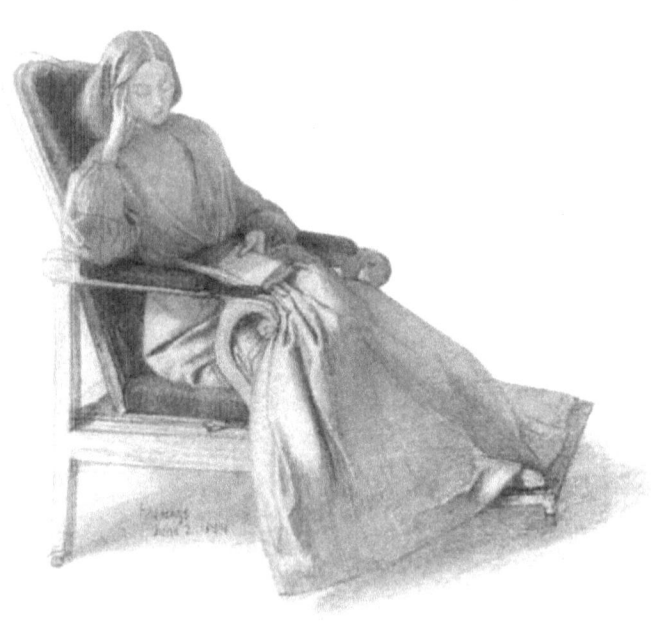

Elizabeth Siddal, 1854

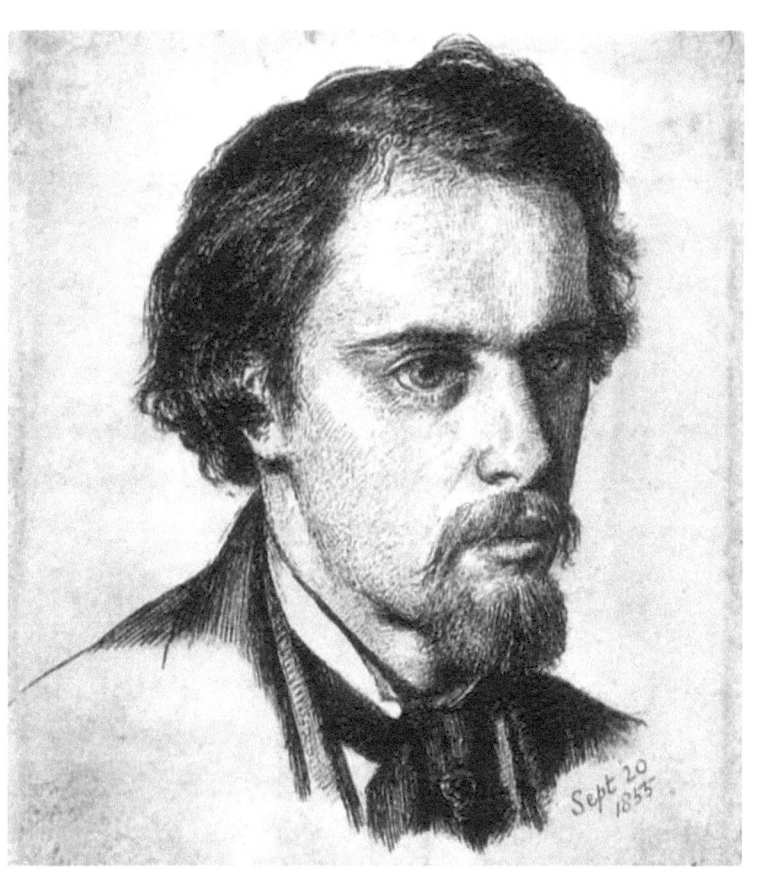

Self Portrait, circa 1855

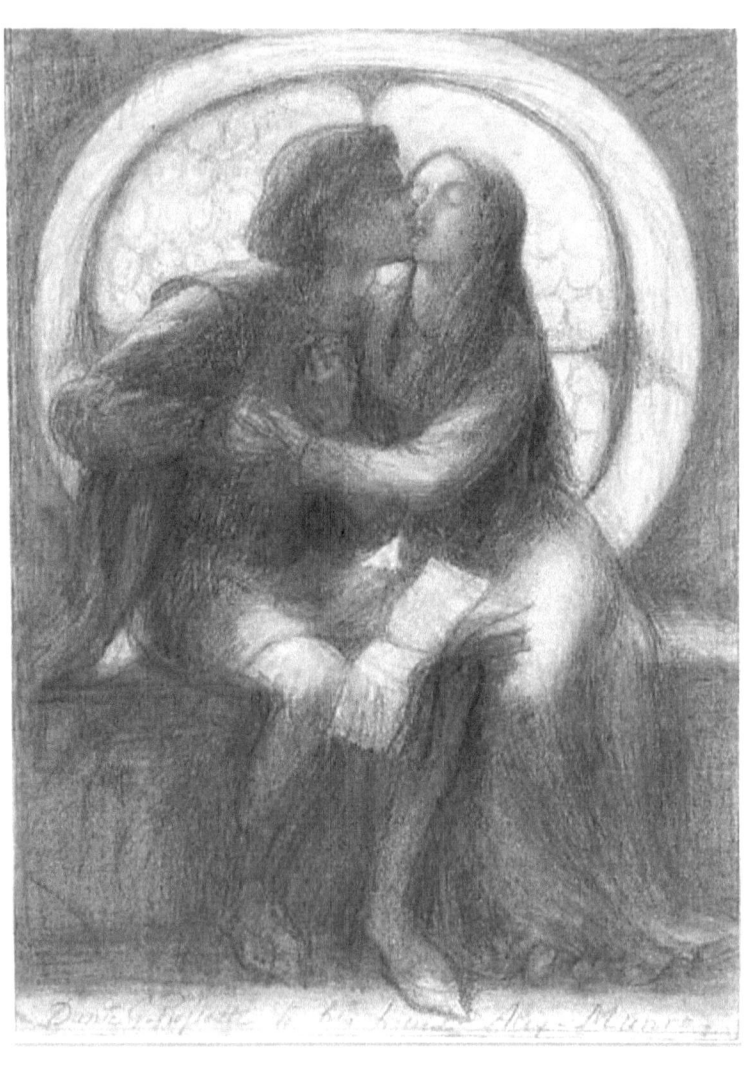

Paolo and Francesca, 1855

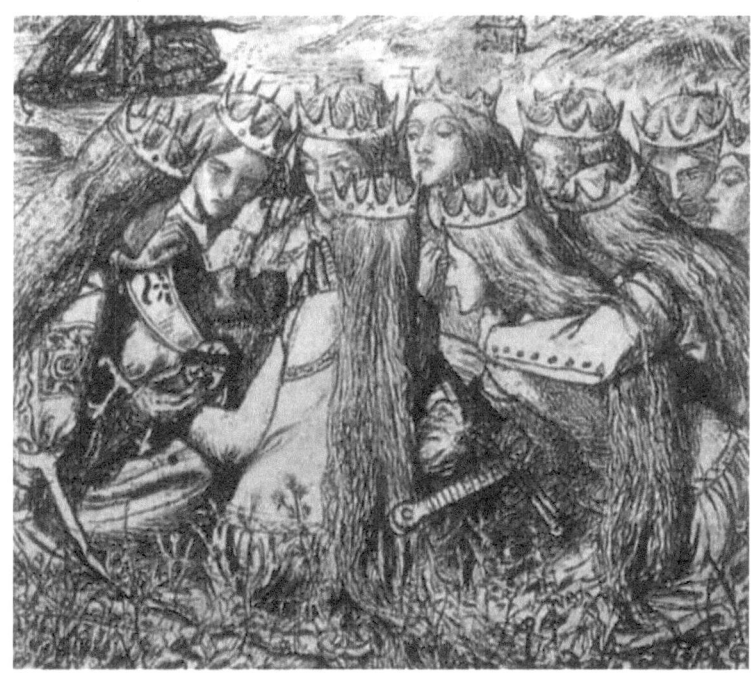

King Arthur and the Weeping Queens, 1856-1857

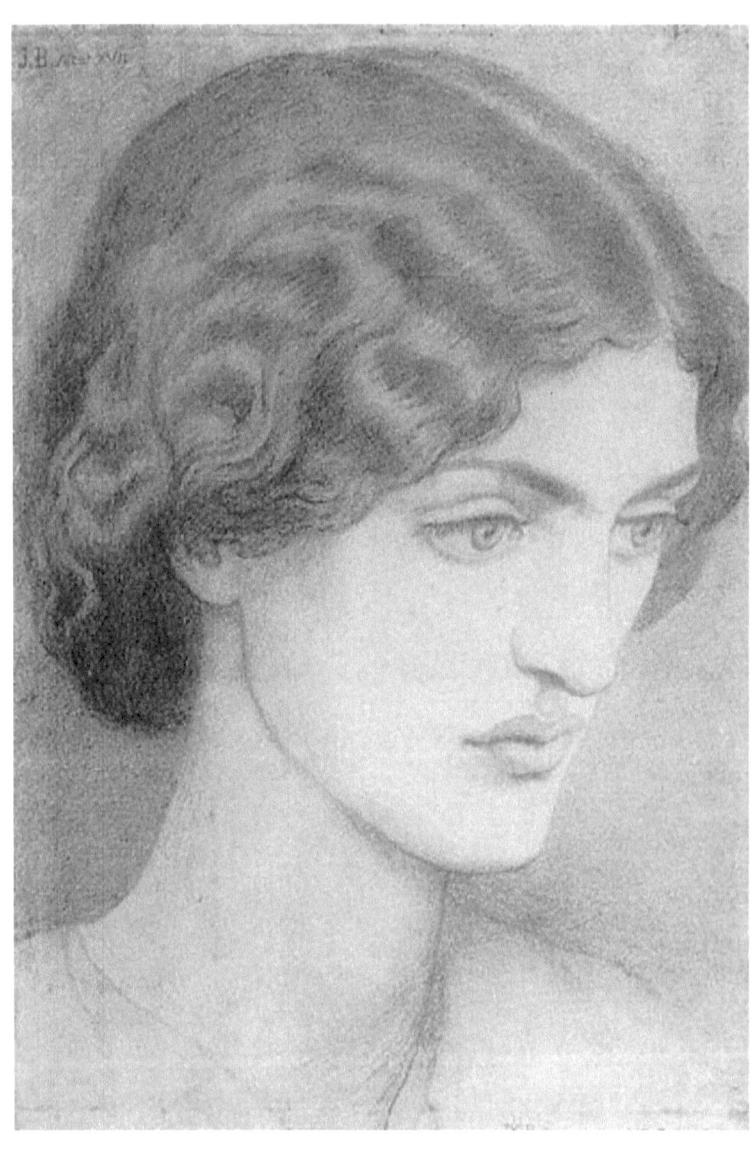

Jane Burden, 1857

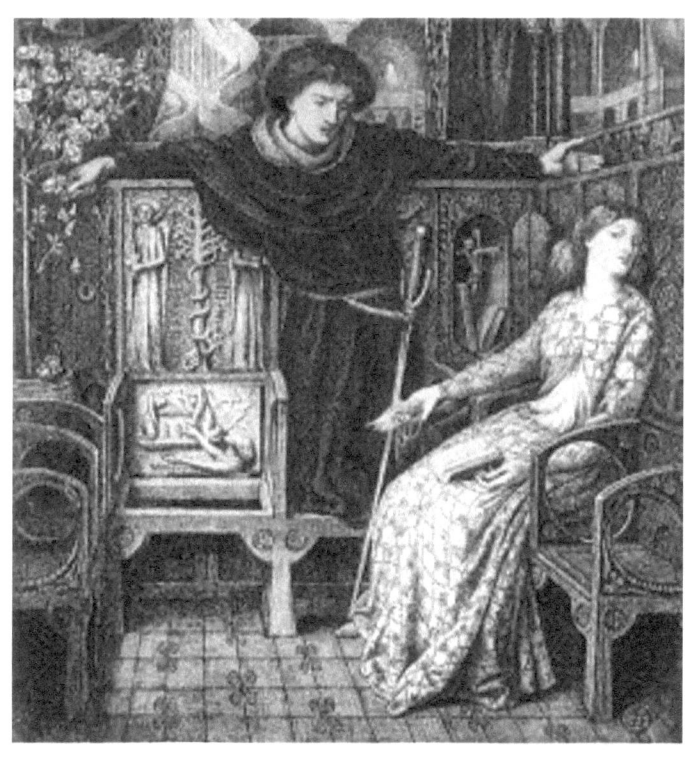

Hamlet and Ophelia, 1858

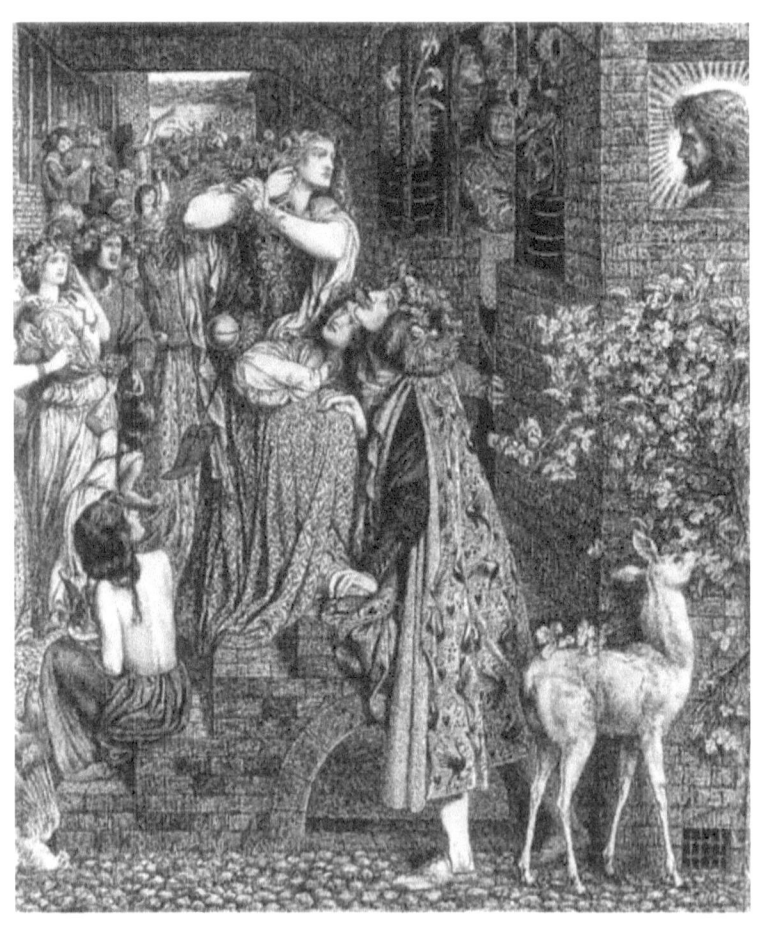

Mary Magdalene at the Door of Simon the Pharisee,
1858

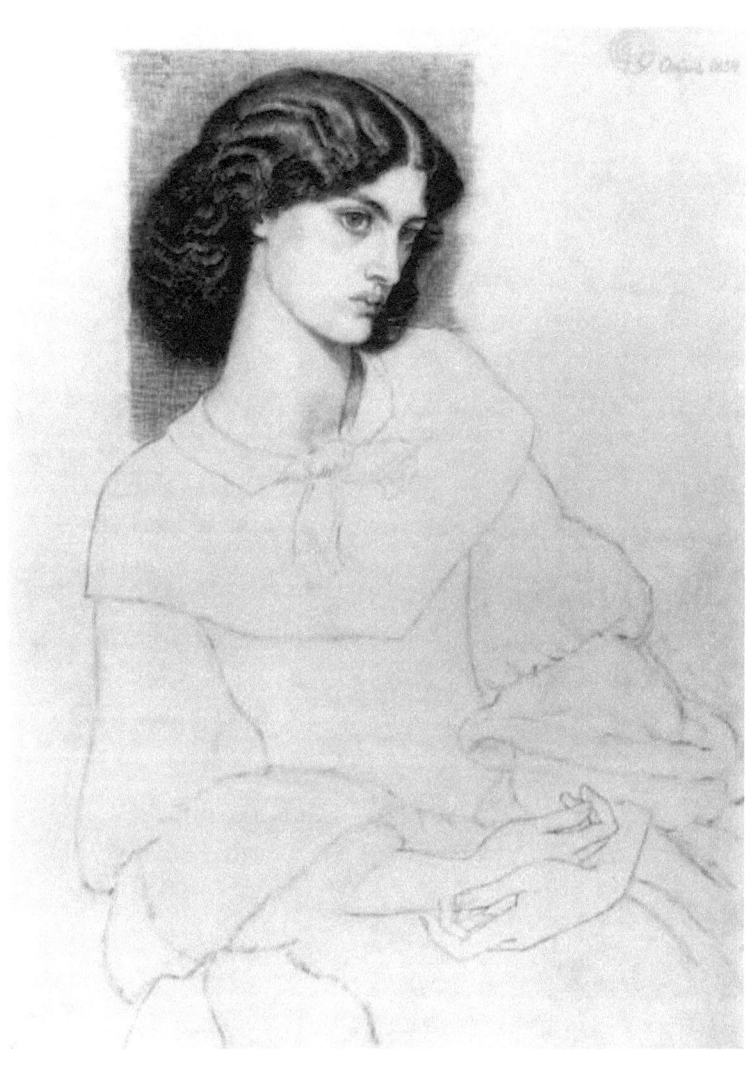

Jane Burden, aged 18, 1858

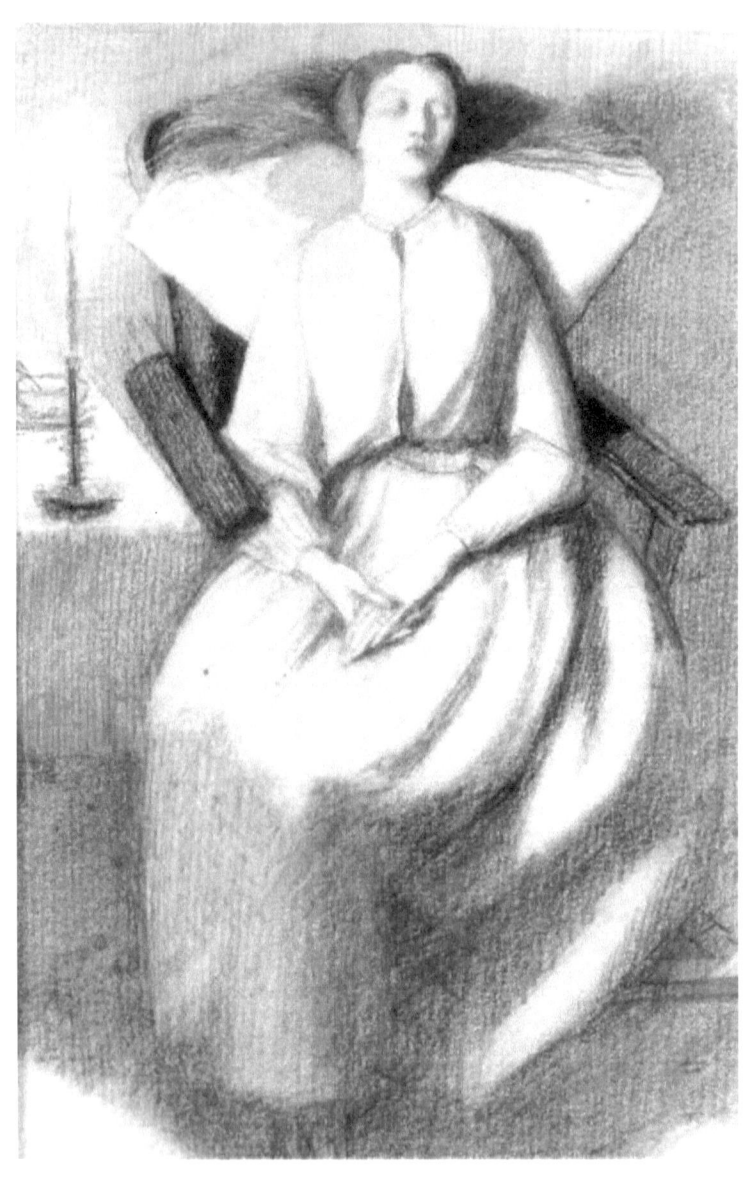

Elizabeth Siddal Seated in a Chair, 1859-1860

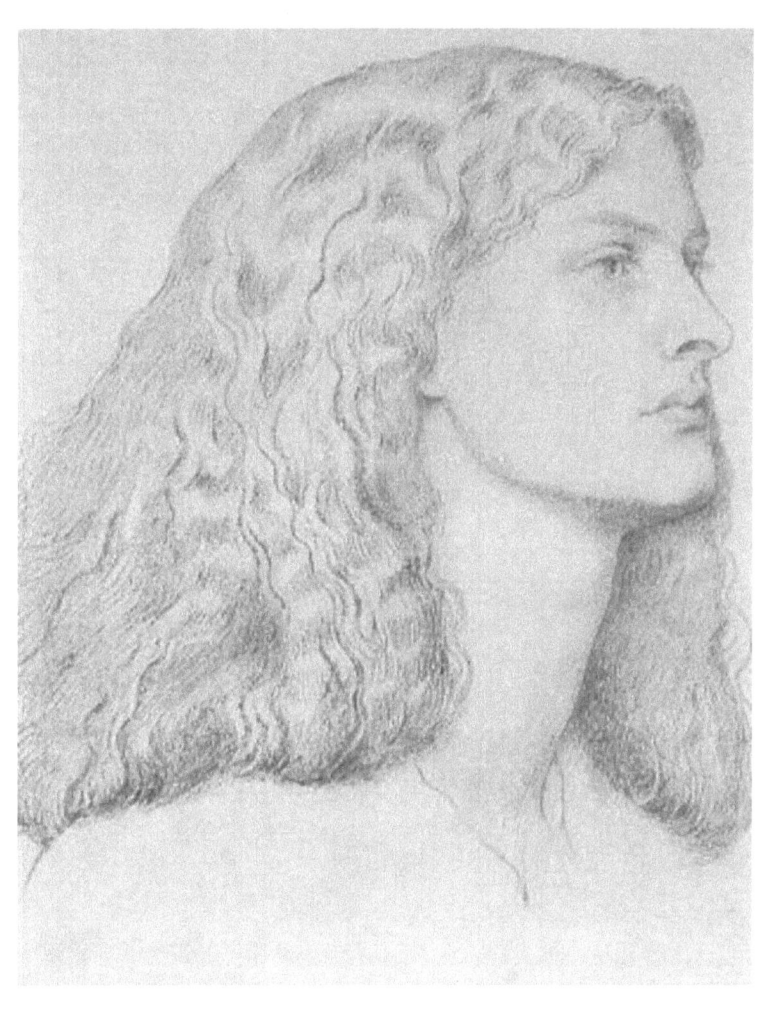

Annie Miller, 1860

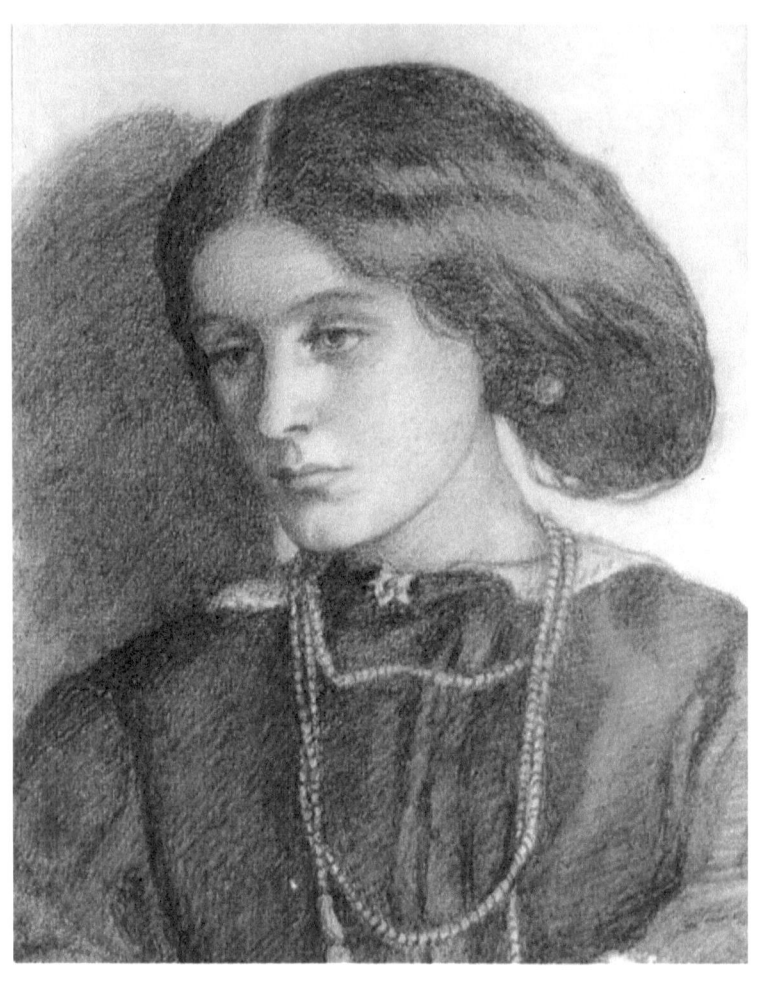

Mrs. Burne-Jones, 1860

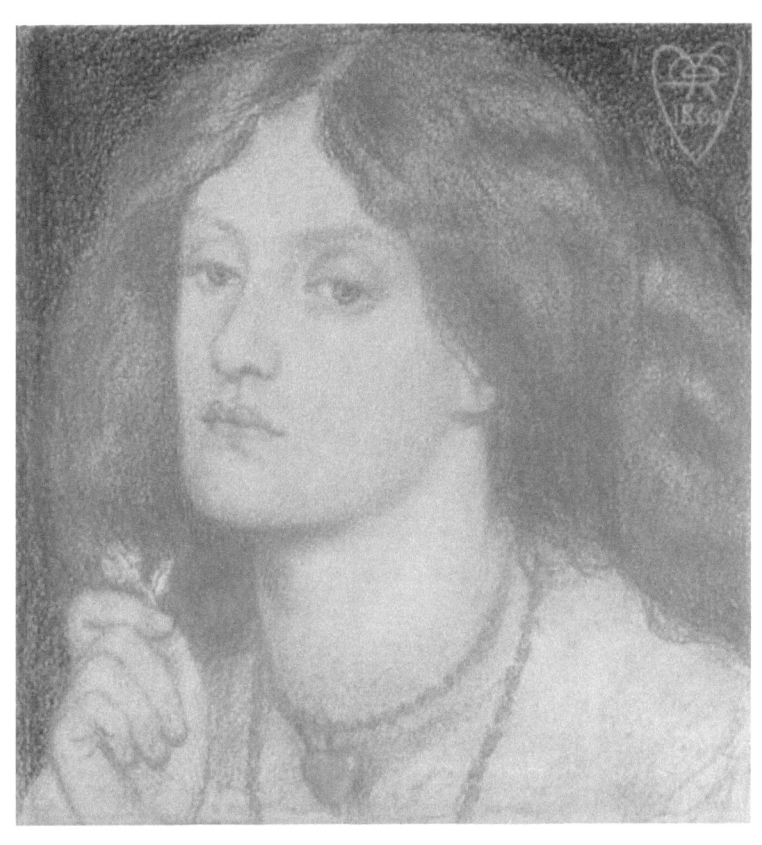

Regina Cordium, 1860

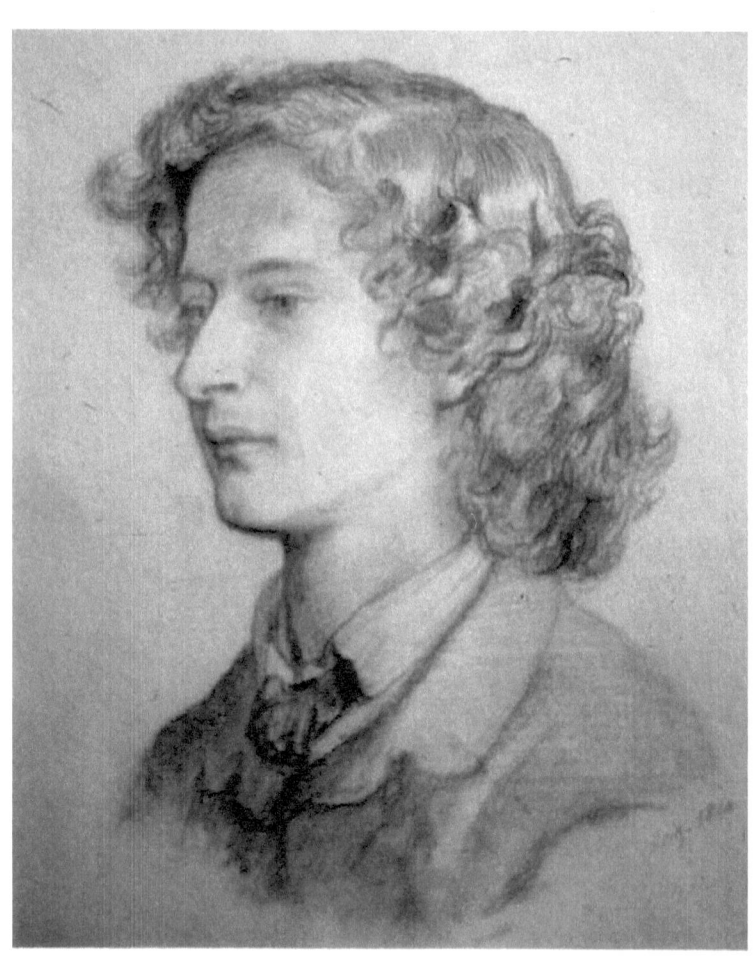

Algernon Charles Swinburne, 1860

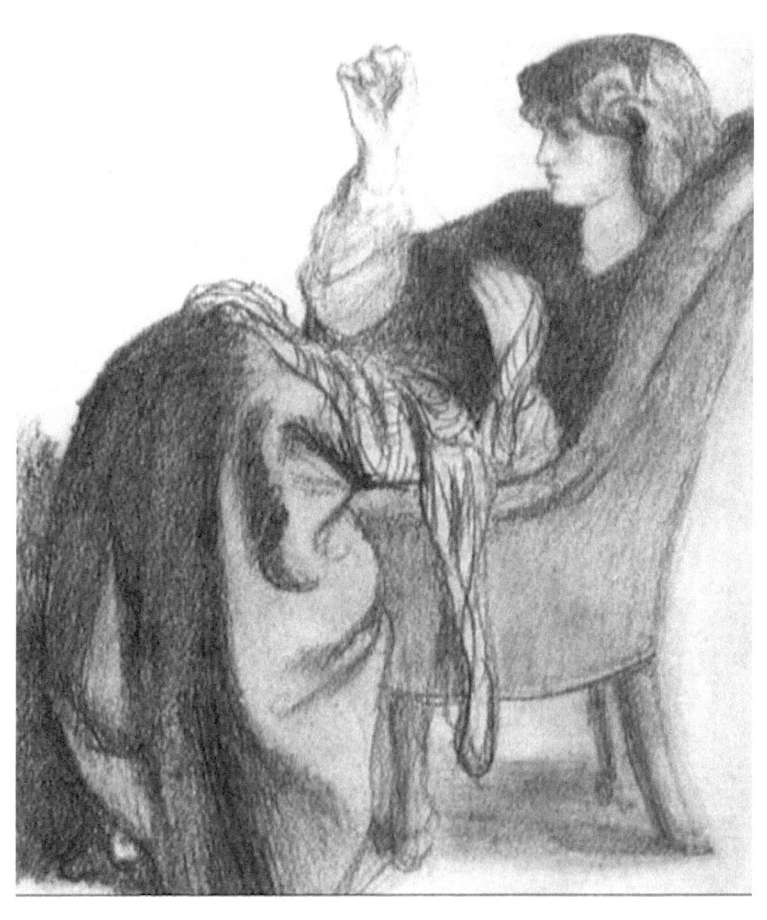

Jane Morris, 1860

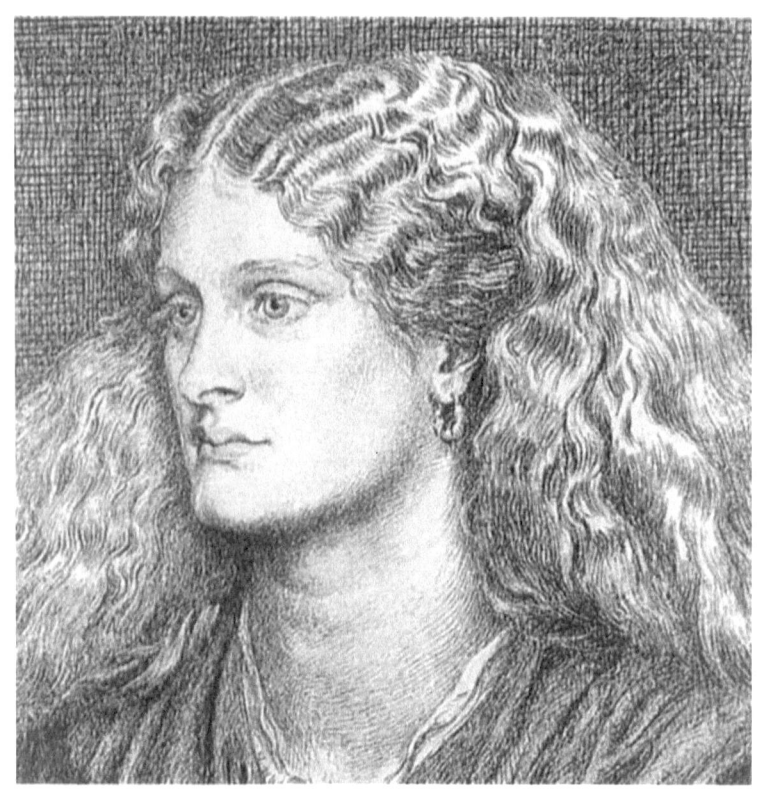

Annie Miller, 1860

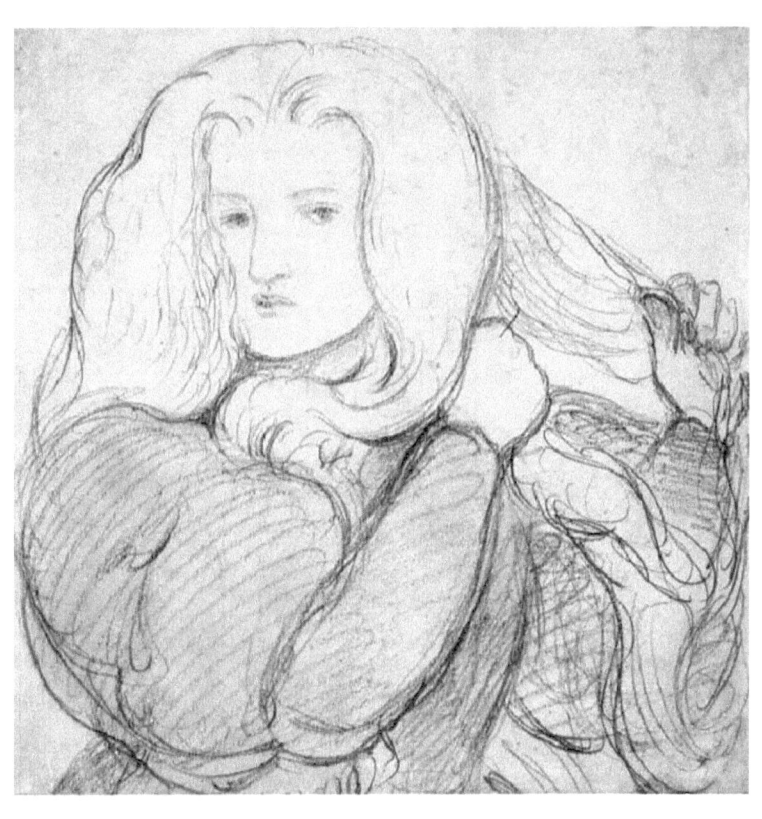

Annie Miller, circa 1860-1863

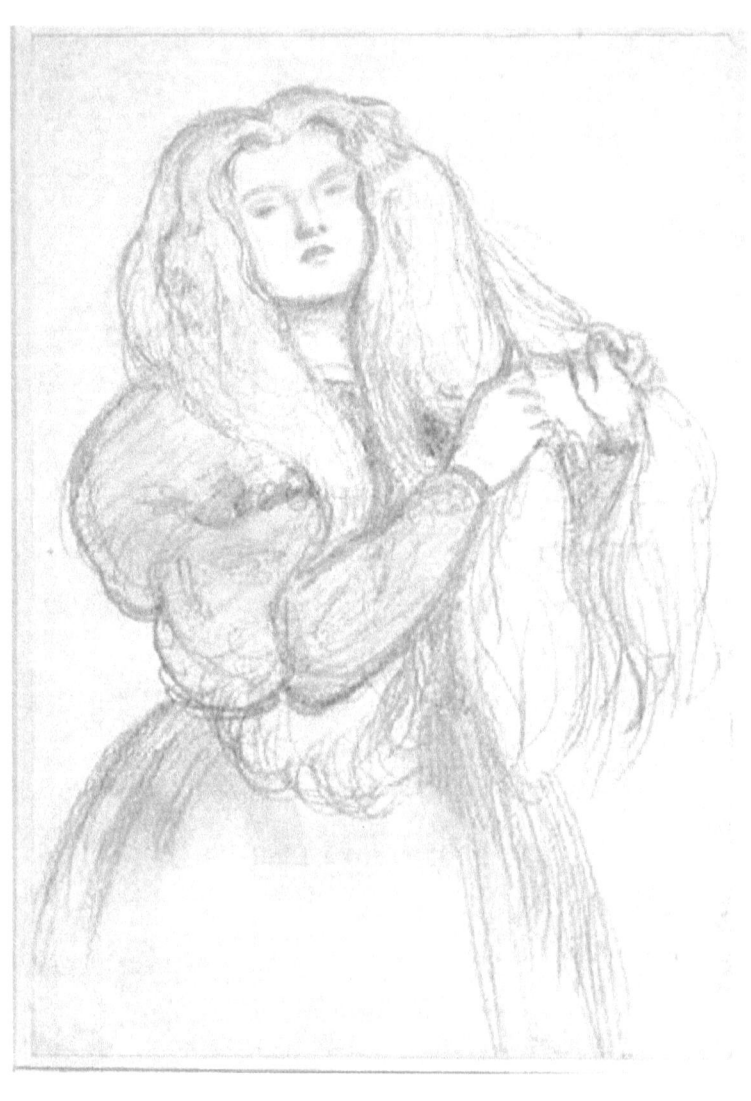

Annie Miller, circa 1860-1863

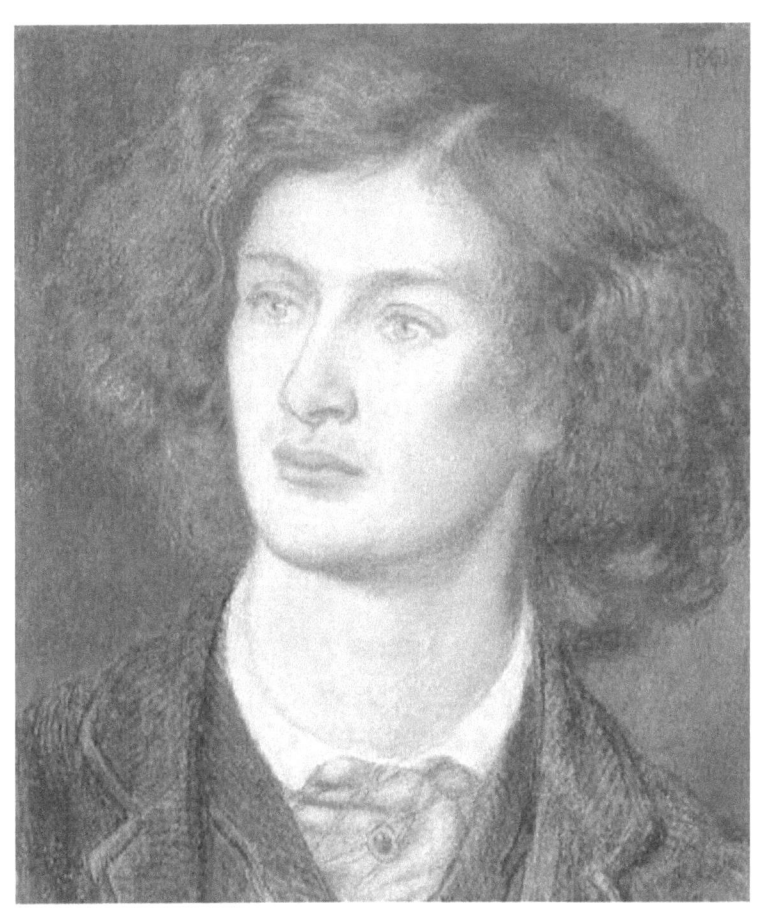

Charles Algernon Swinburne, 1861

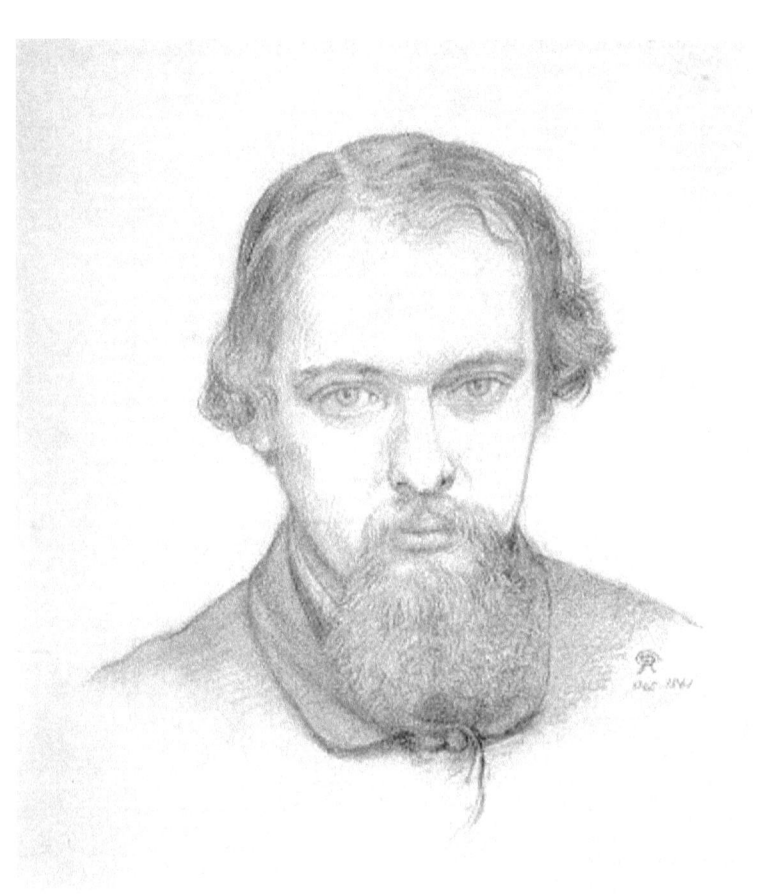

Self Portrait, 1861

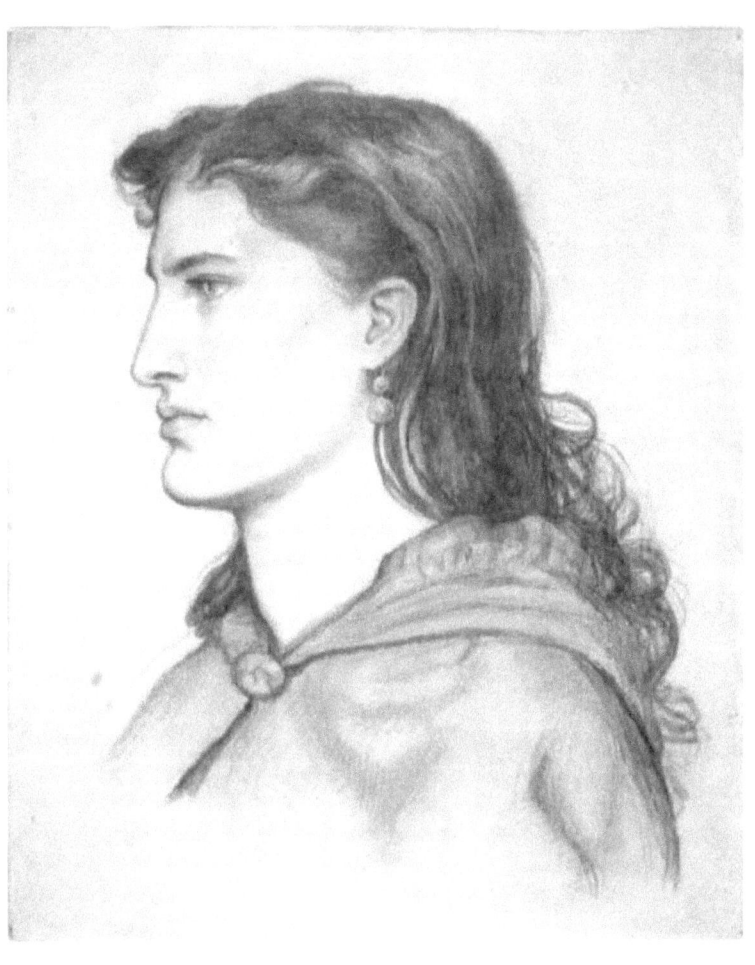

Aggie, 1862

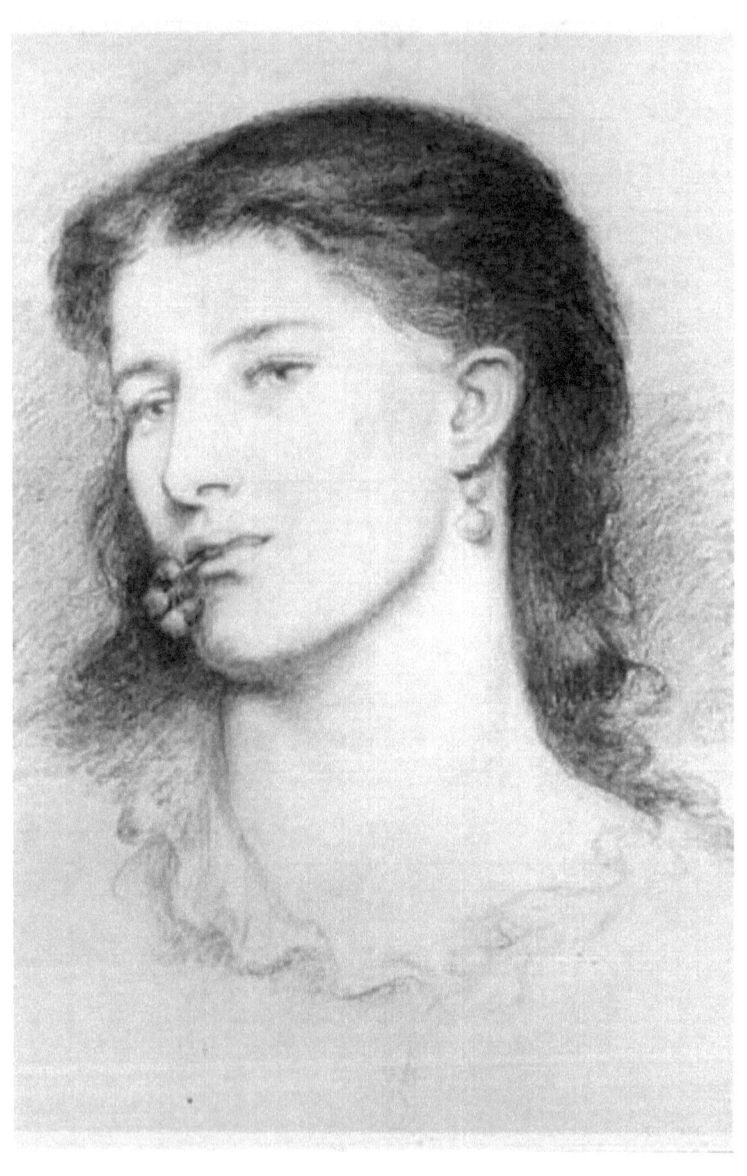

Aggie, 1862

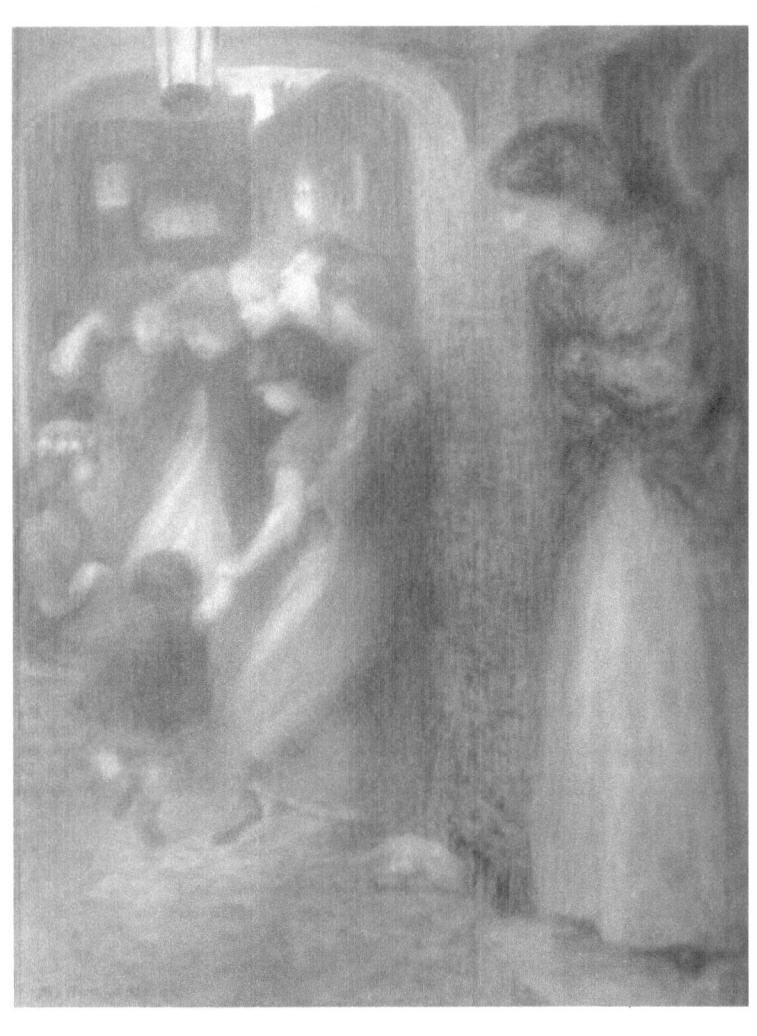

The Gate of Memory, 1864

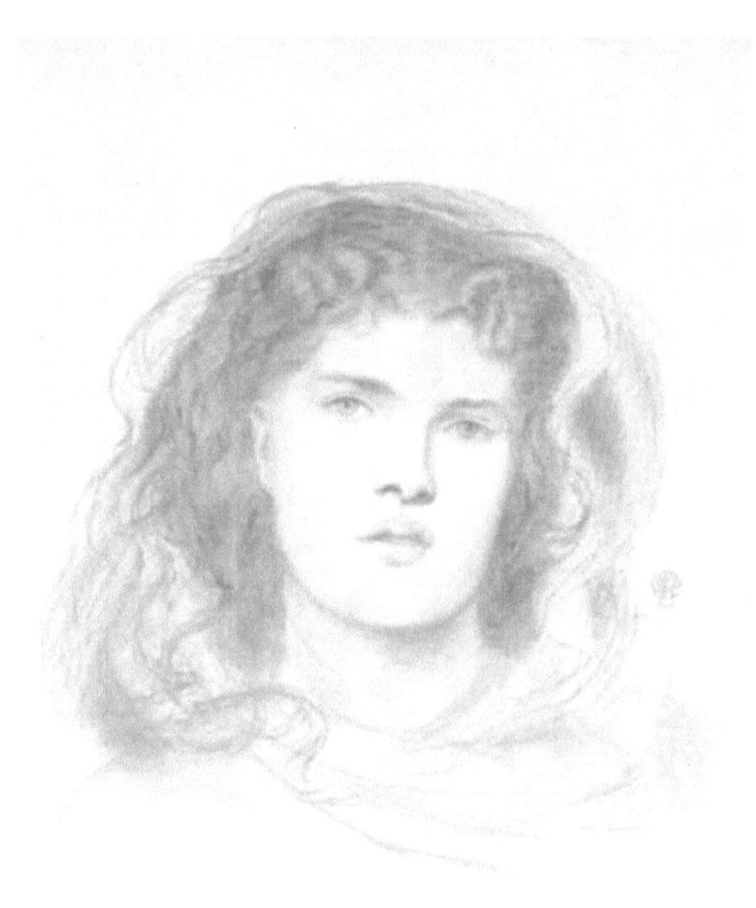

The Beloved - study (also known as The Bride - study), 1865

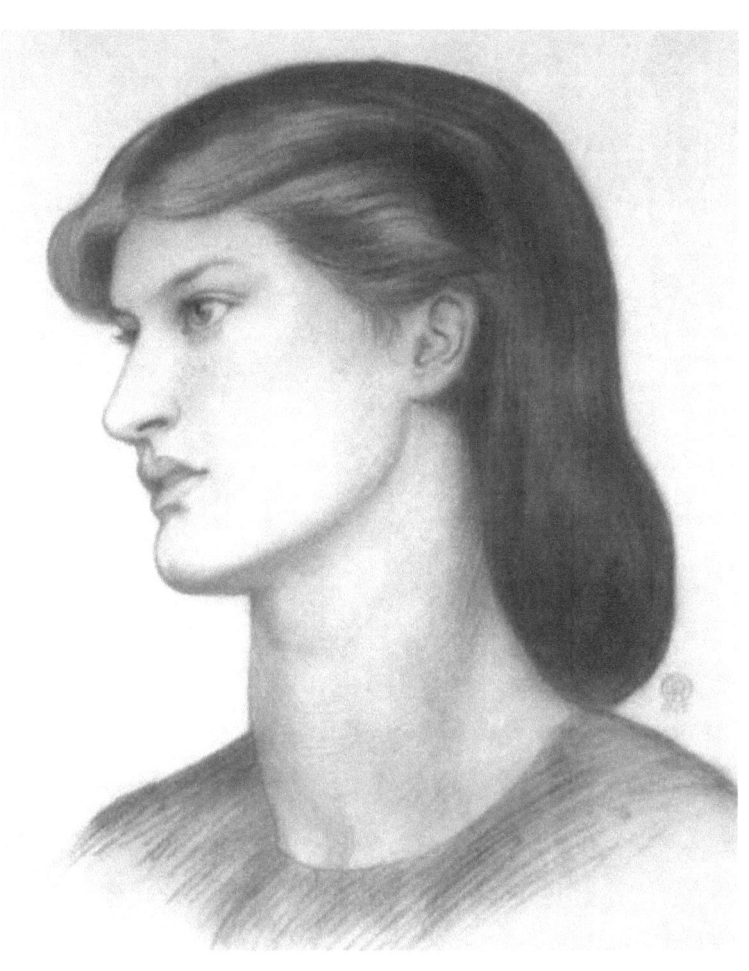

Alexa Wilding, circa 1865, chalk

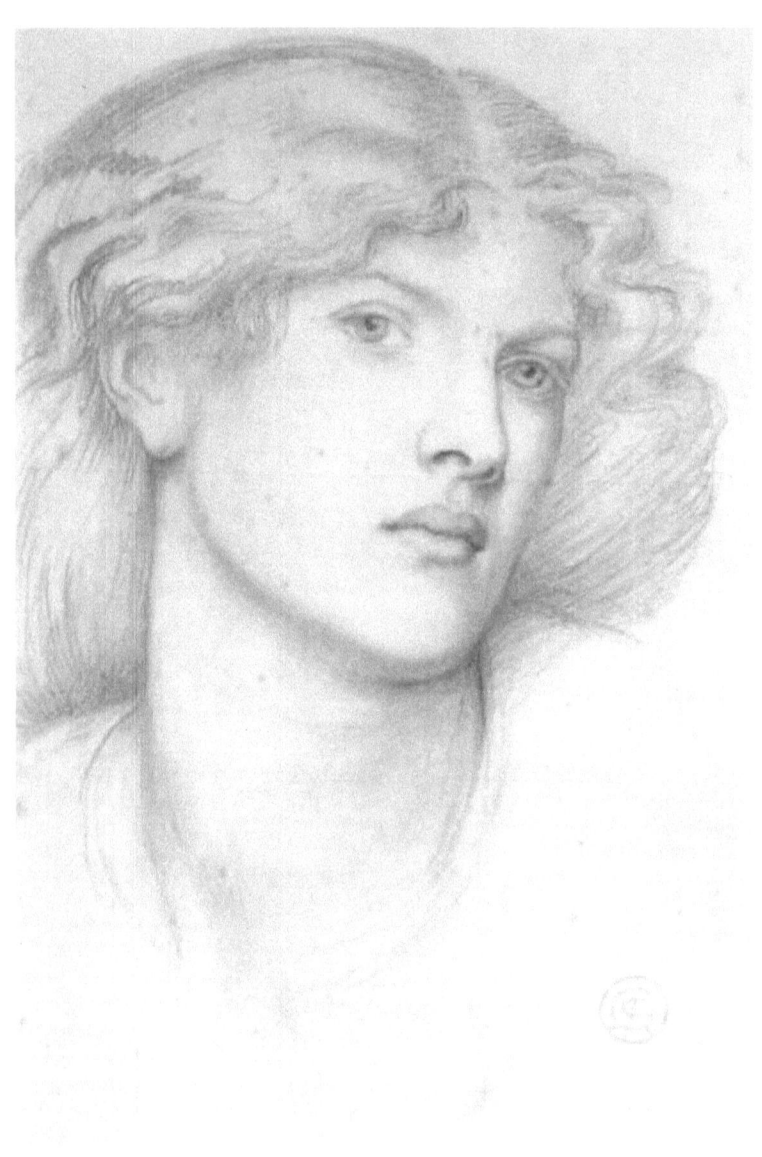

Fanny Cornforth, circa 1865

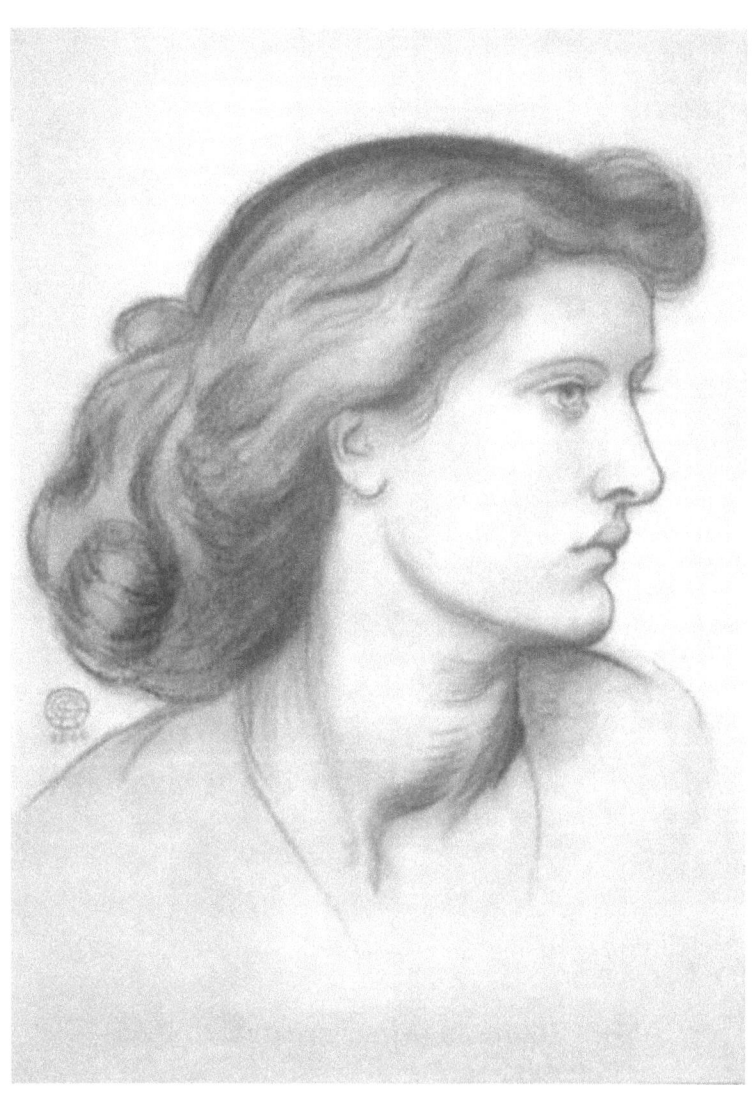

Alexa Wilding (also known as Alice Wilding), 1866

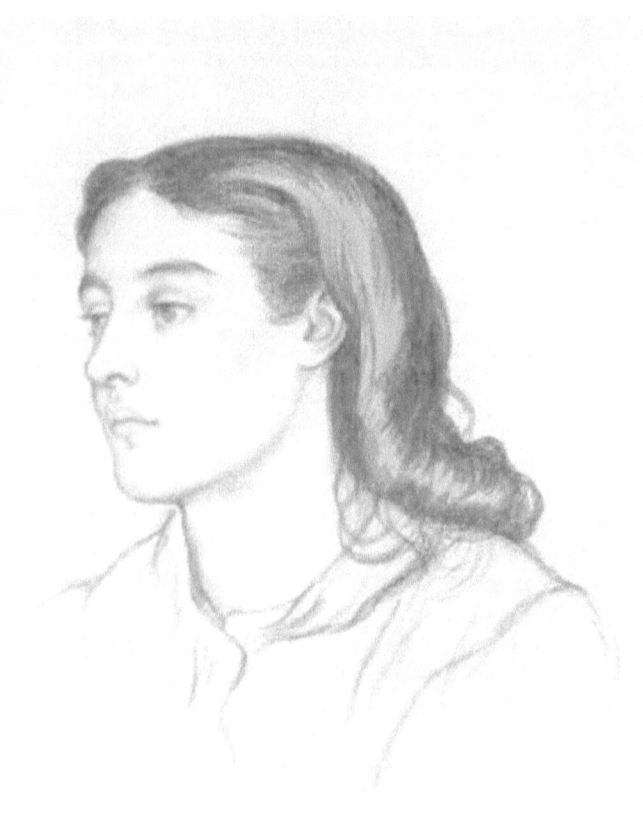

Miss Robinson (Mrs. Fernandez), 1866

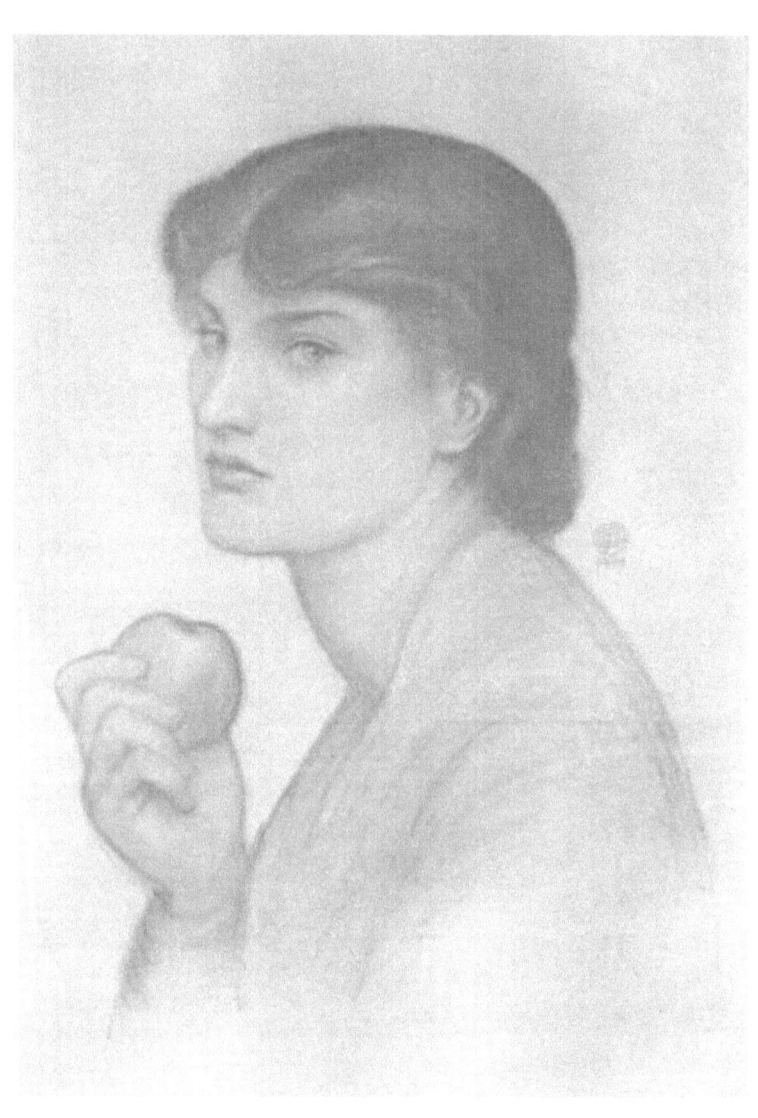

Alexa Wilding Holding an Apple, 1866

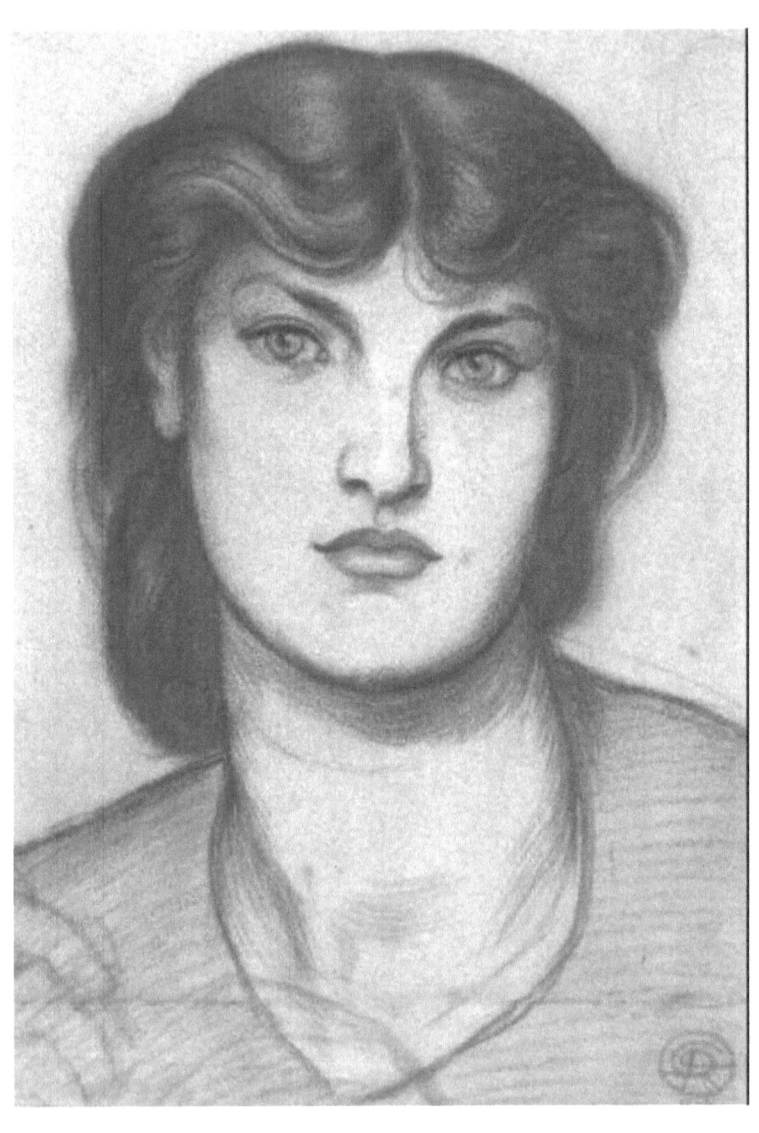

Regina Cordium - study, circa 1866

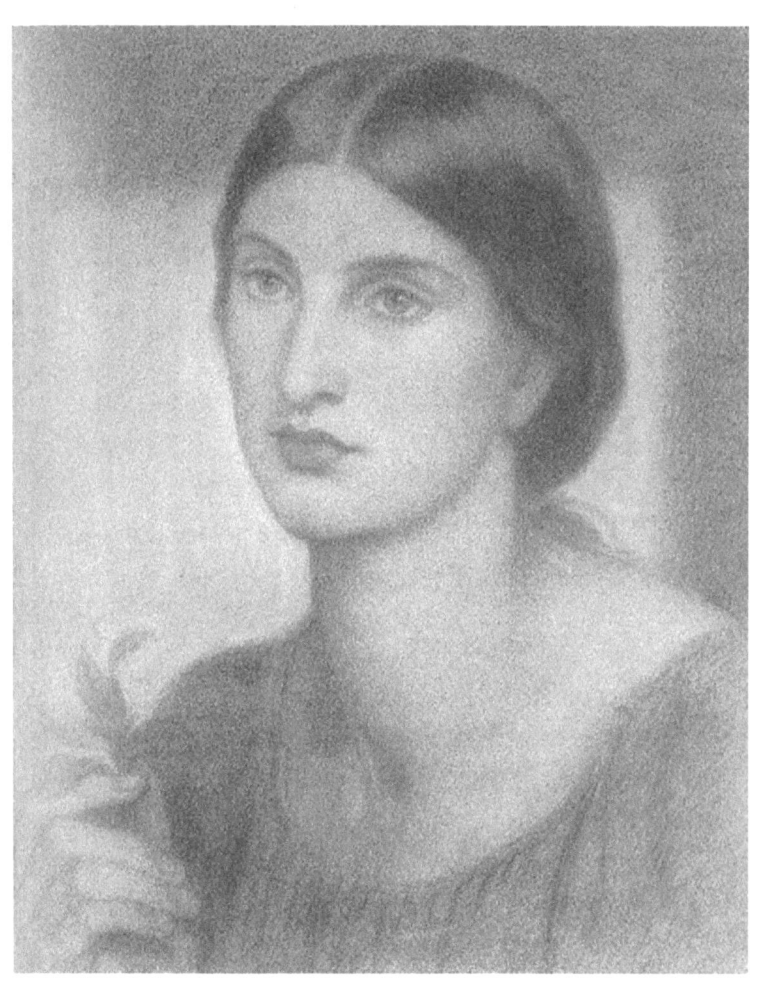

Study of a Girl, 1867

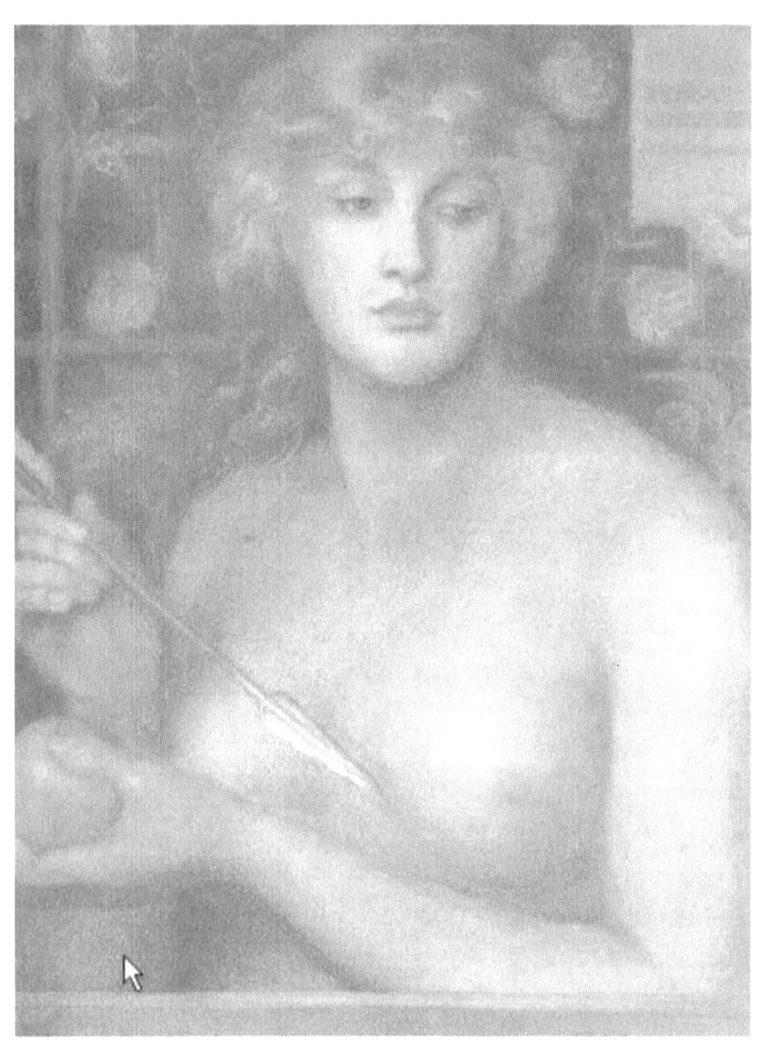

Venus Verticordia - study, 1867

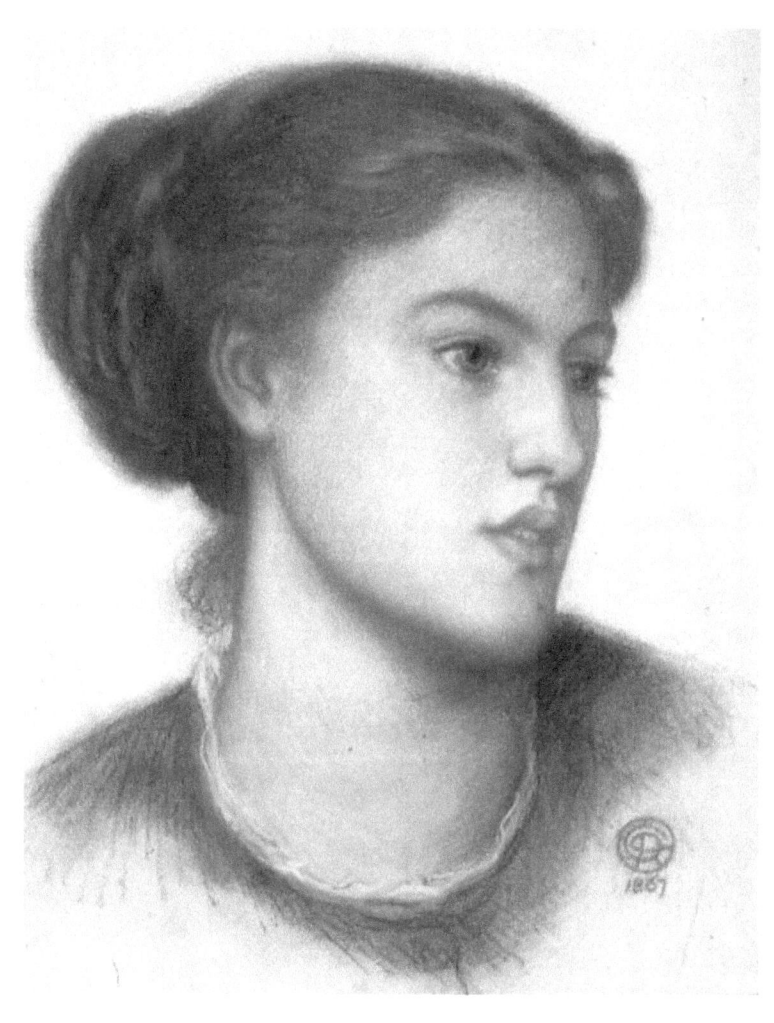

Ellen Smith, 1867

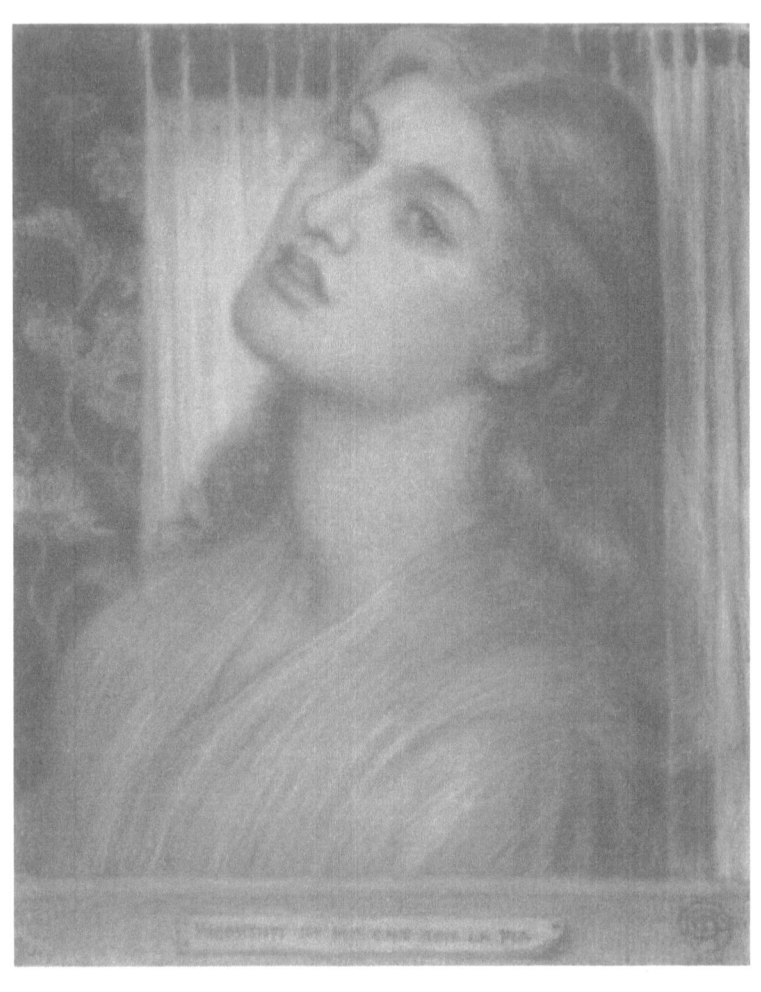

La Pia De' Tolomei - study, 1868

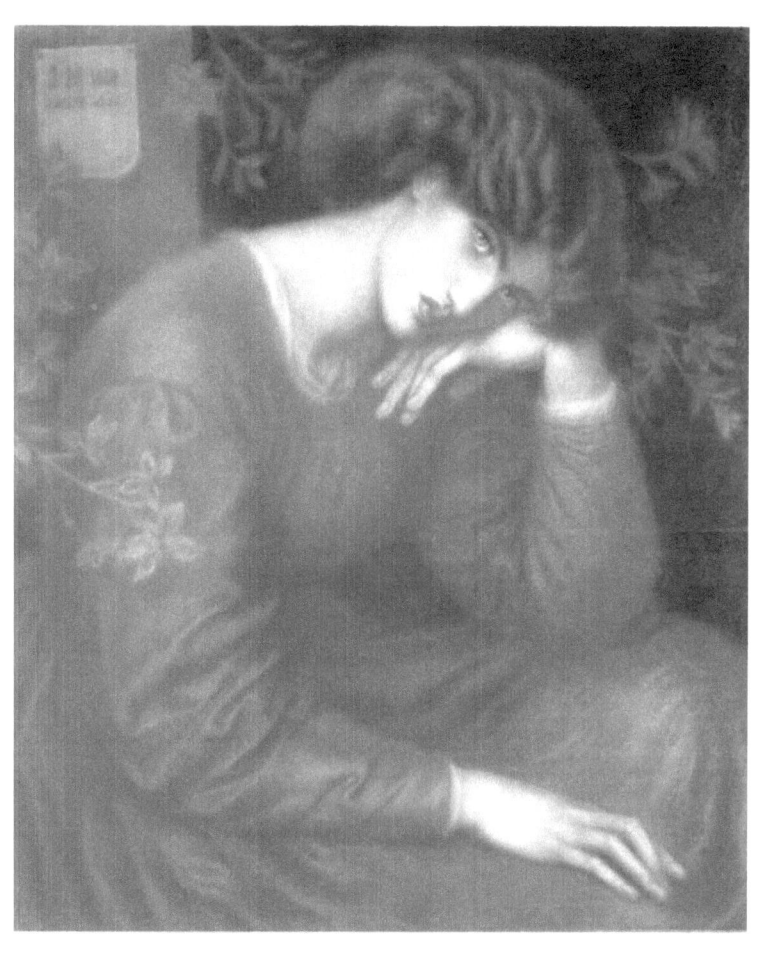

Reverie, 1868

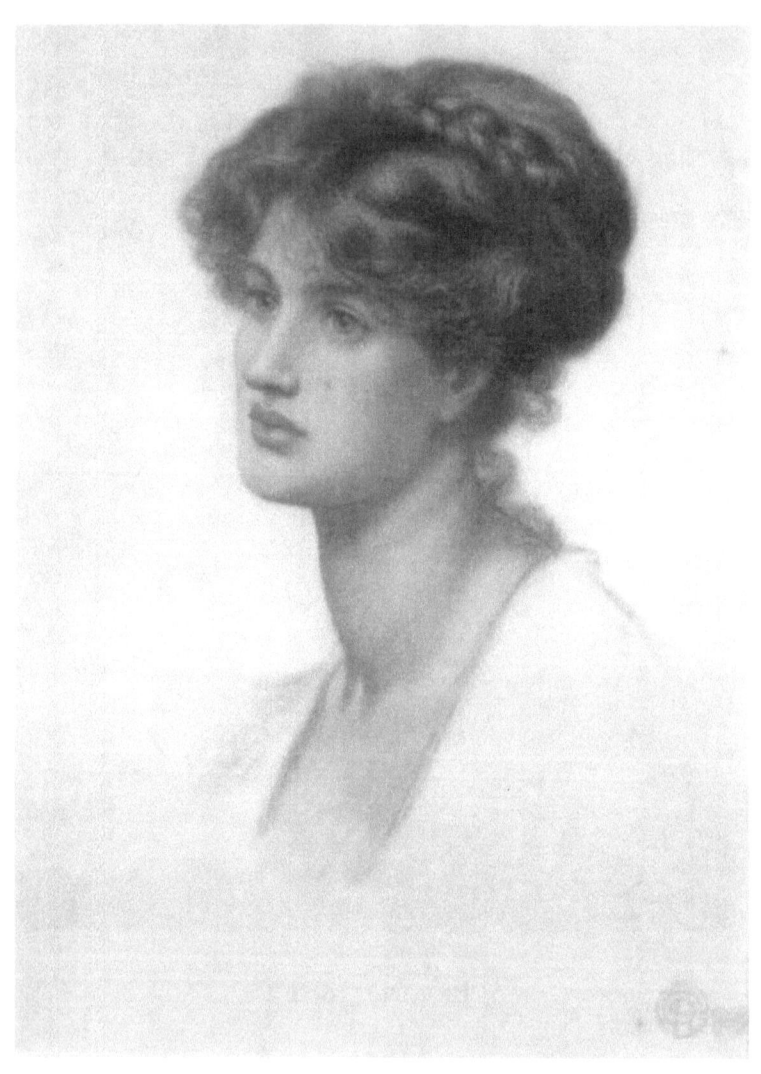

Marie Stillman, 1869

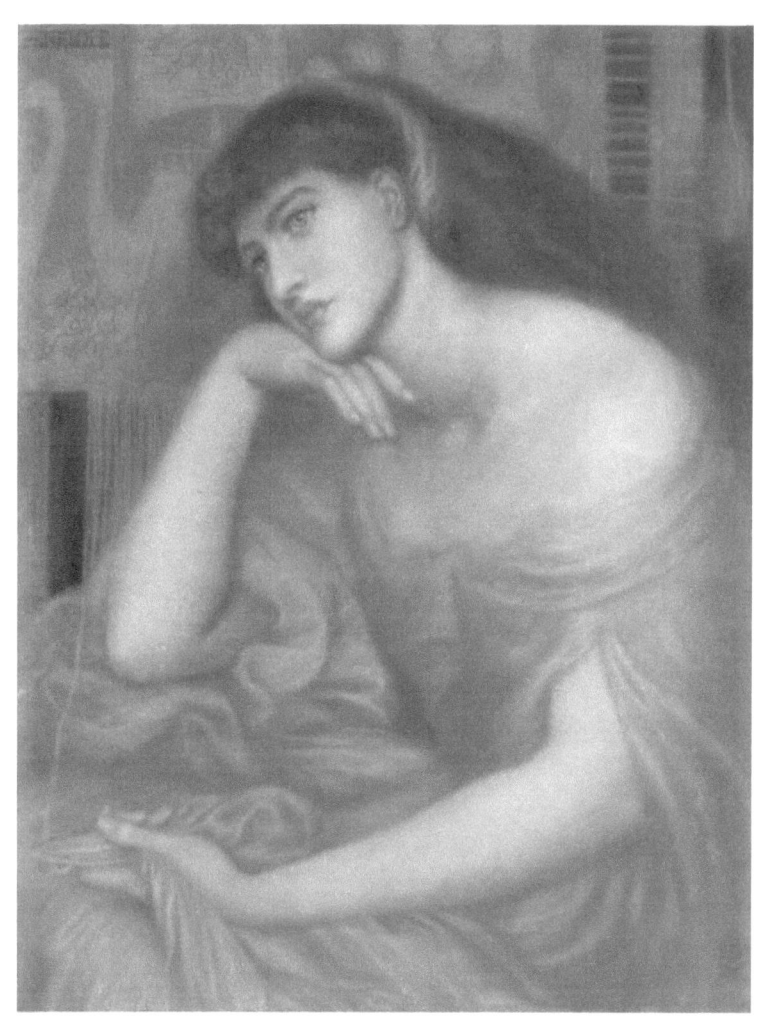

Penelope, 1869

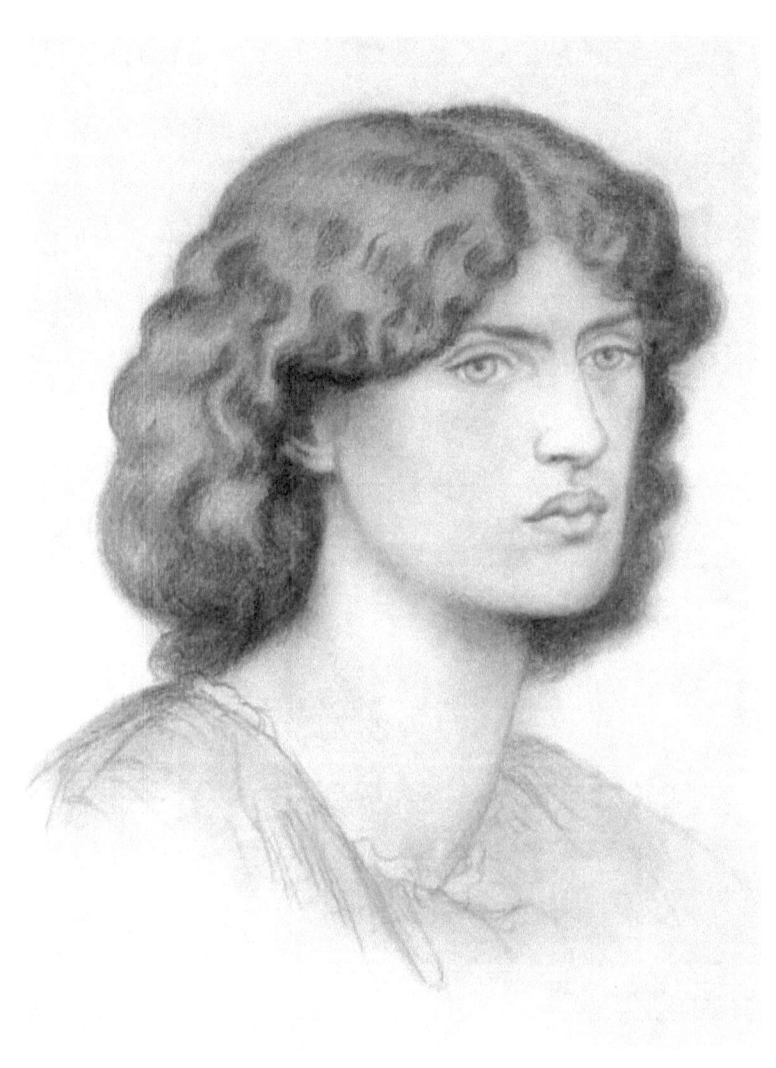

Jane Morris, 1869-1870

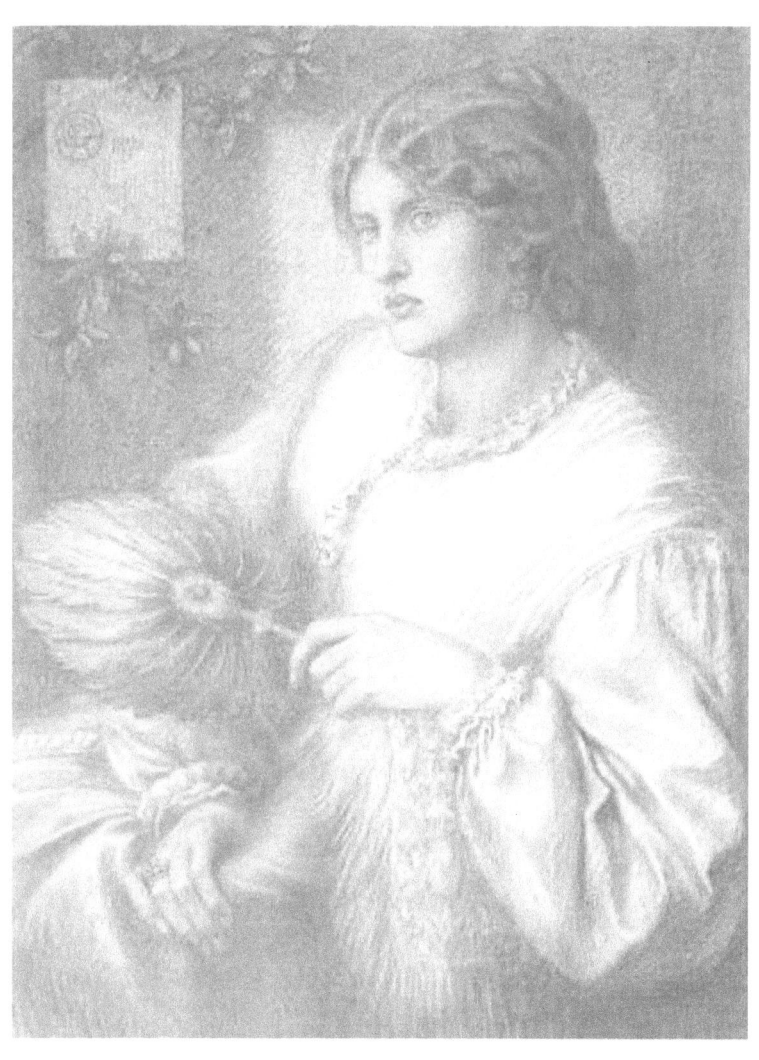

Woman with a Fan, 1870

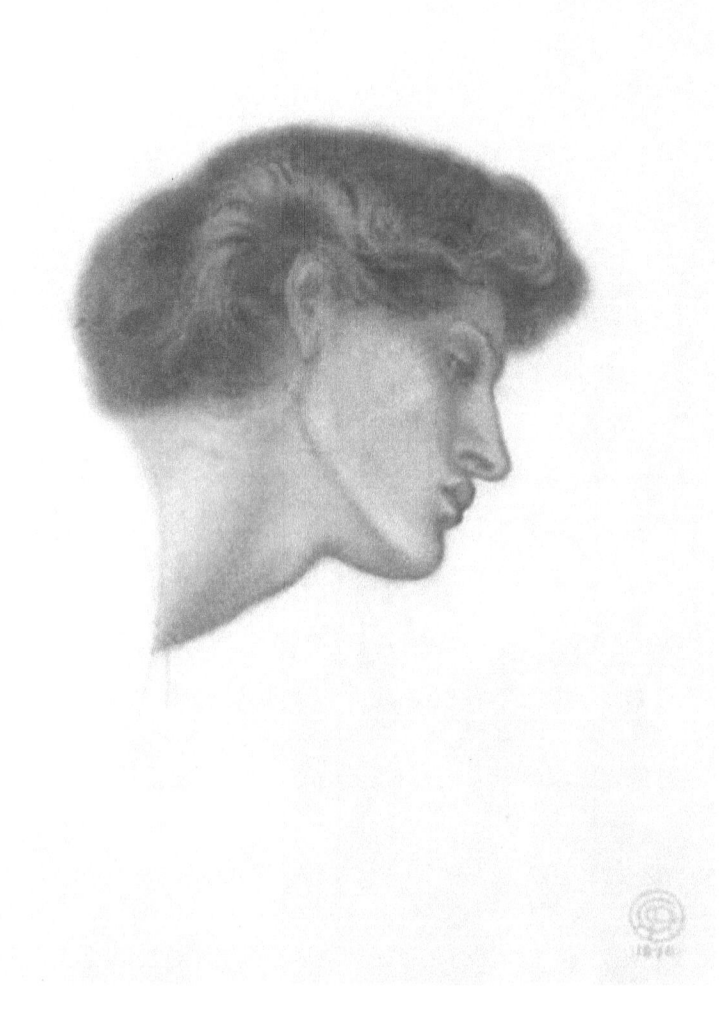

Dante's Dream at the Time of the Death of Beatrice - study, 1870

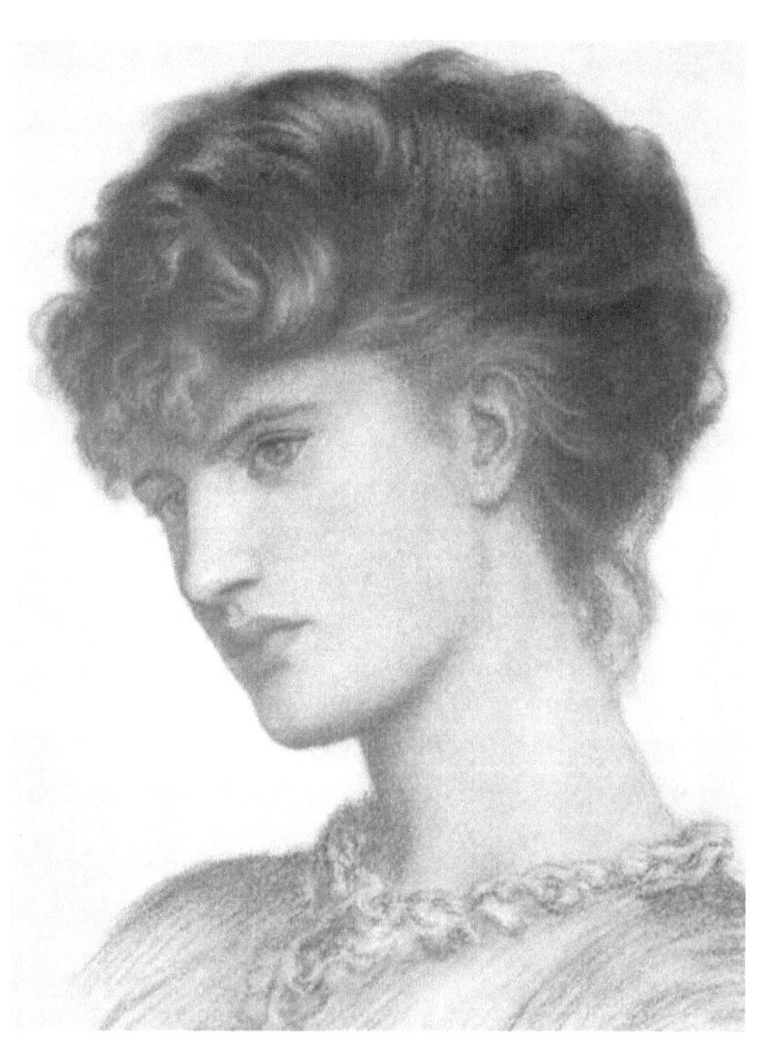

Portrait of a Lady, 1870

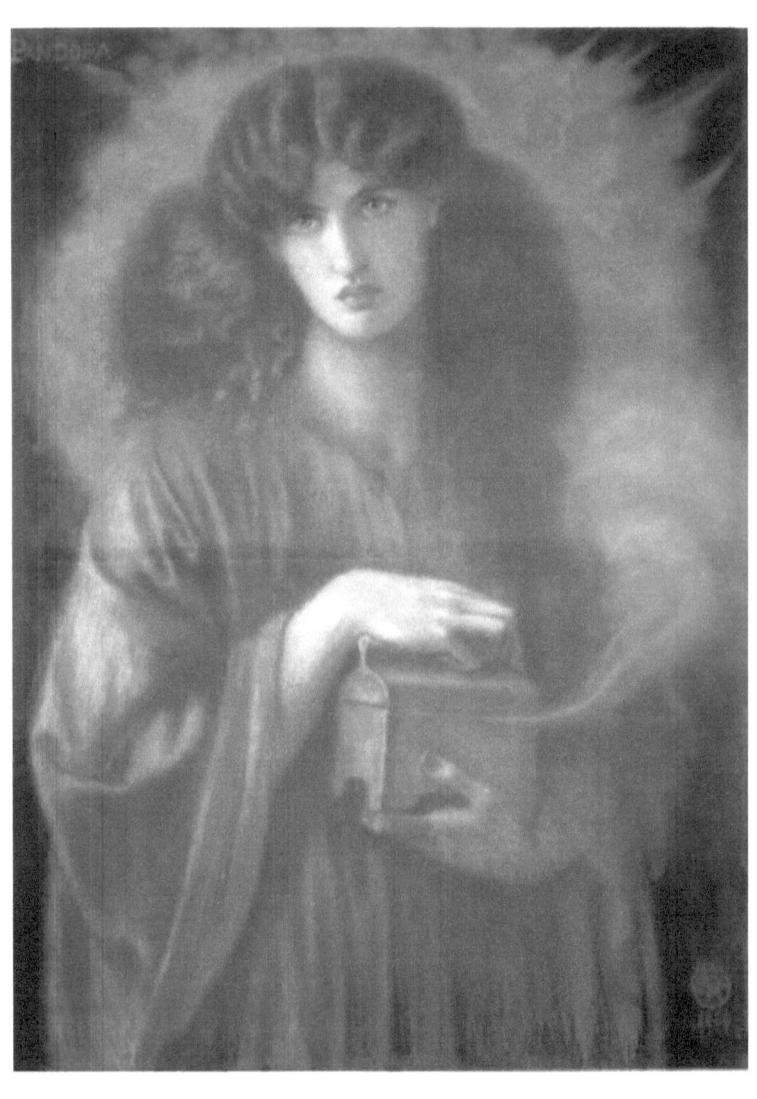

Pandora, 1870, chalk

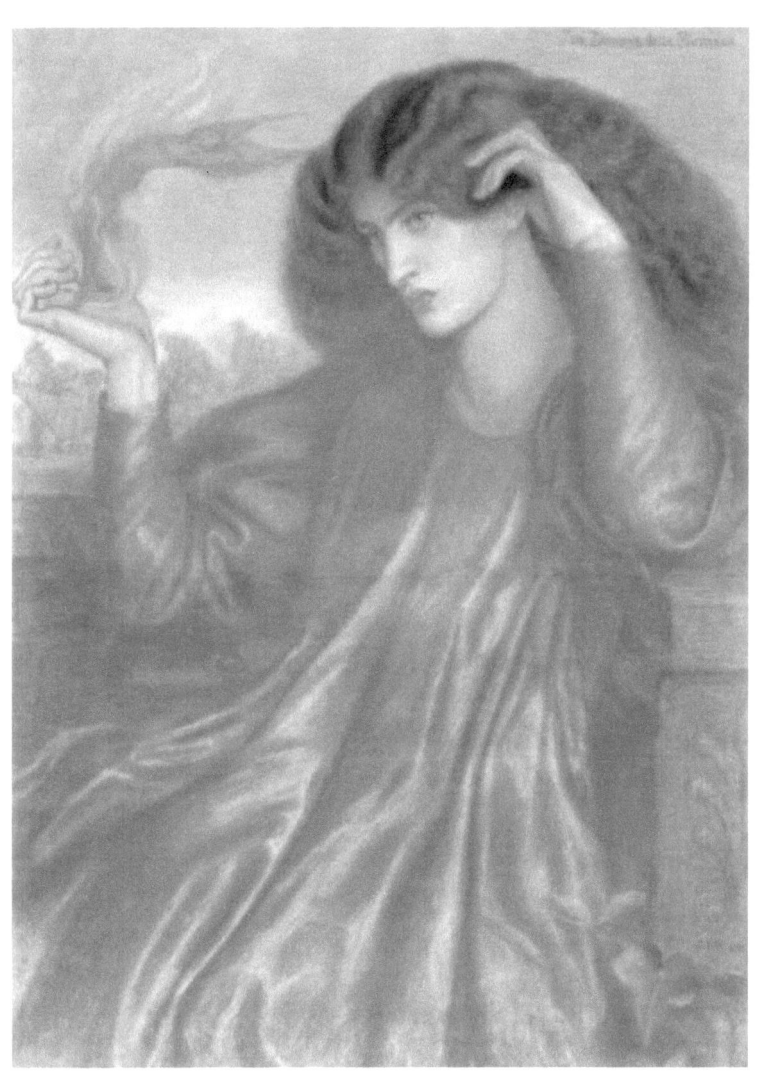

La Donna della Fiama, 1870

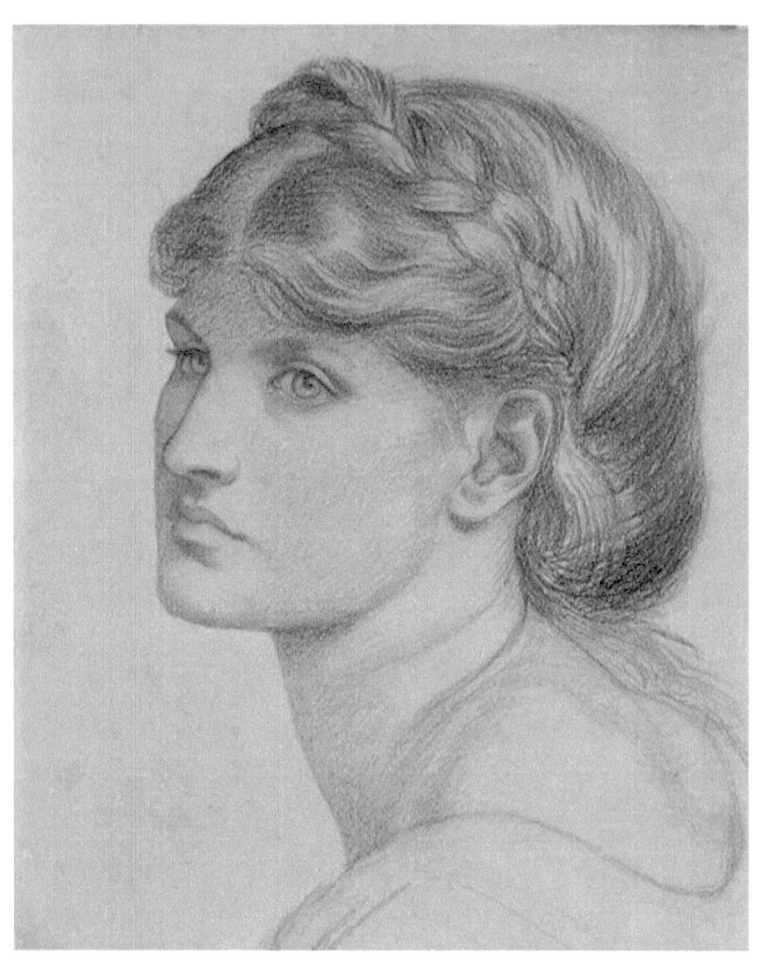

The Bower Meadow - study, 1871-1872

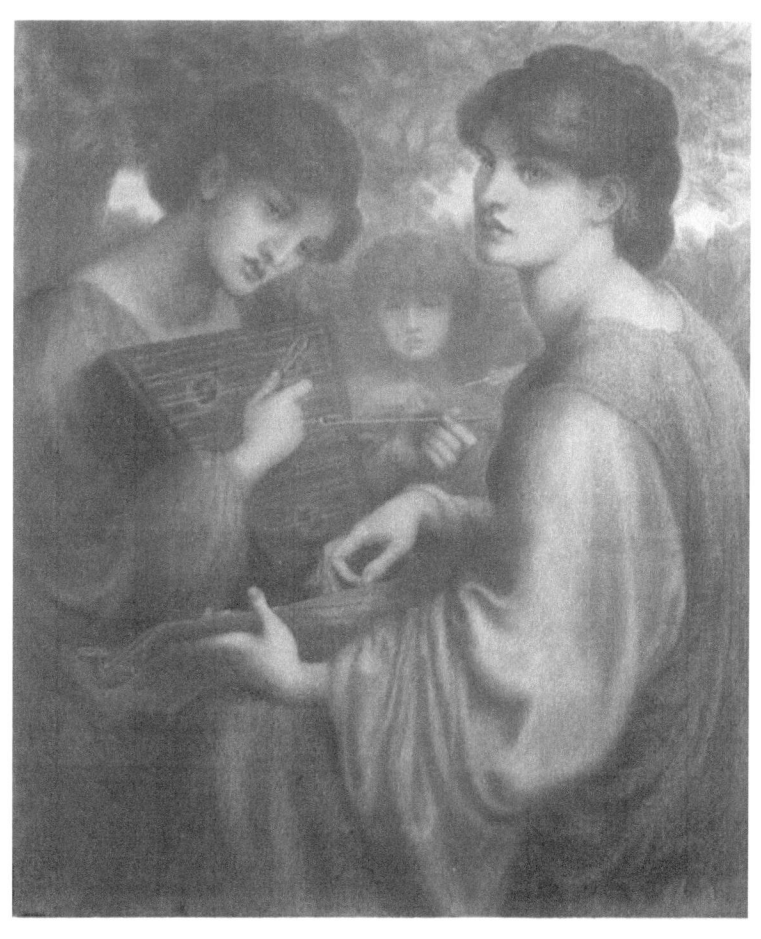

The Bower Meadow - study, circa 1871-1872

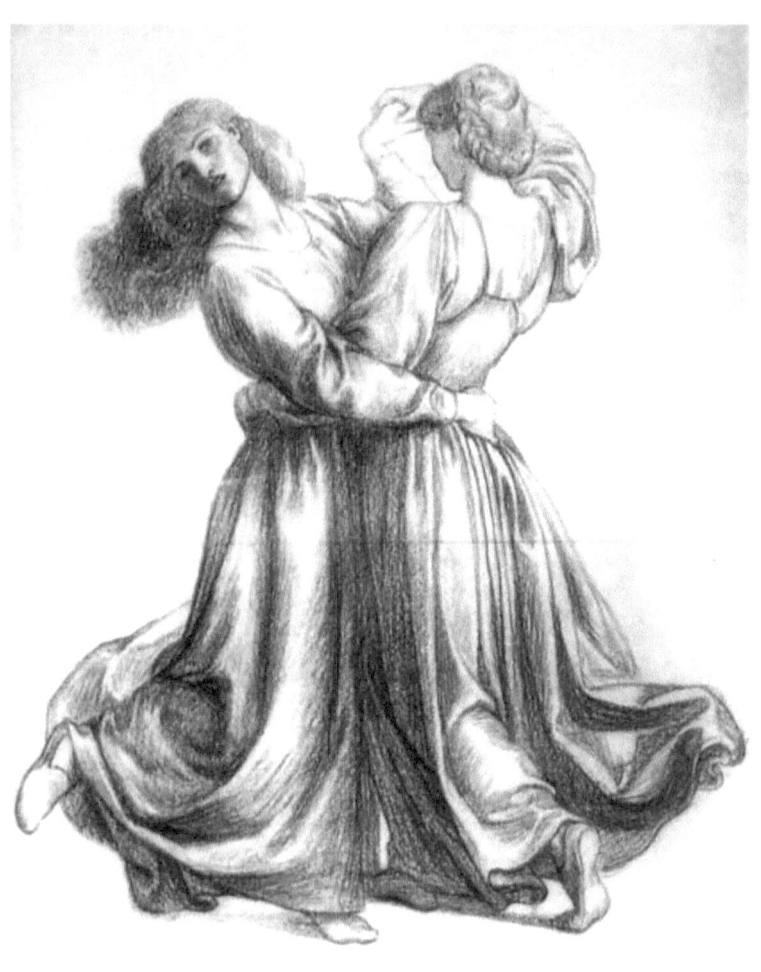

The Bower Meadow - Study (also known as Study of
Dancing Girls), 1872

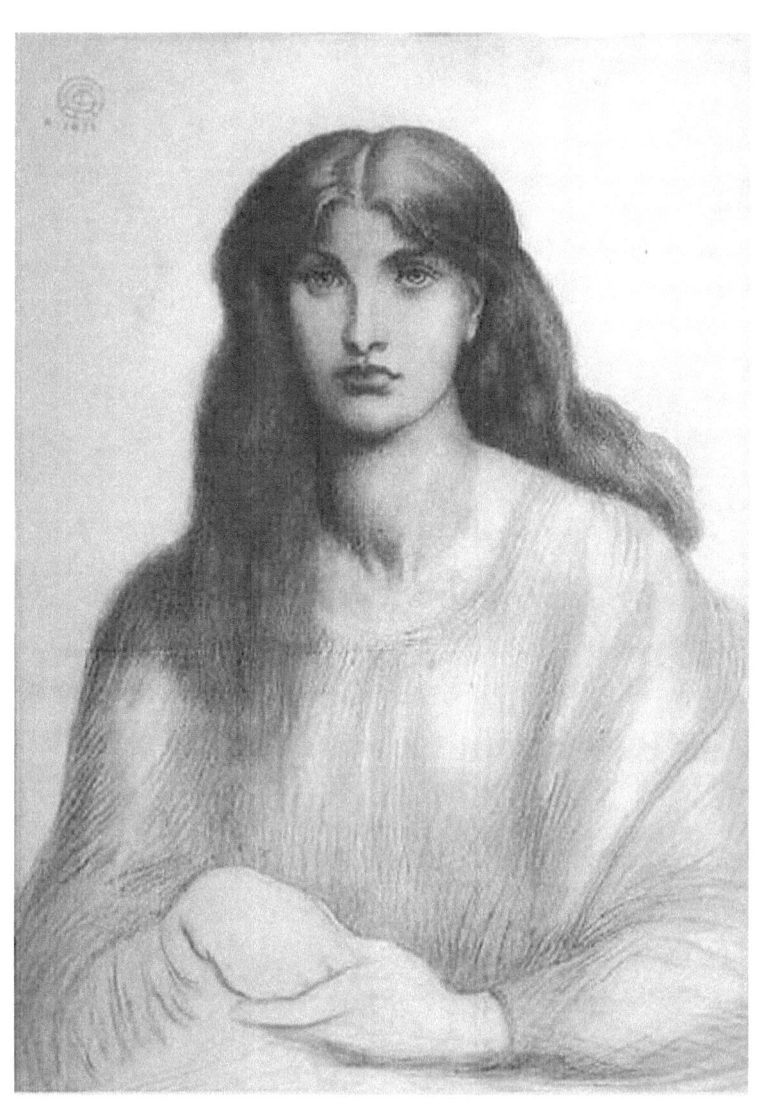

Alexa Wilding, 1872

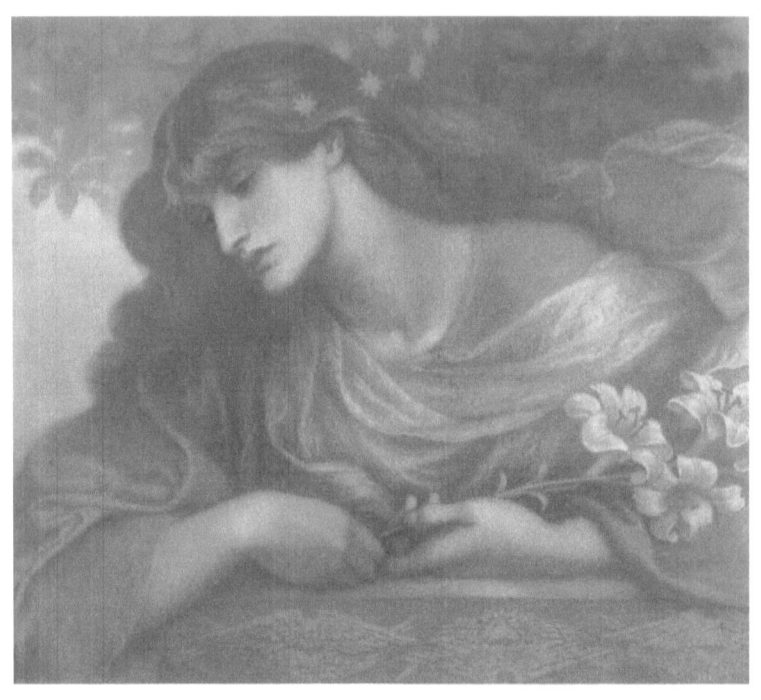

The Blessed Damozel - Study, 1873, chalk

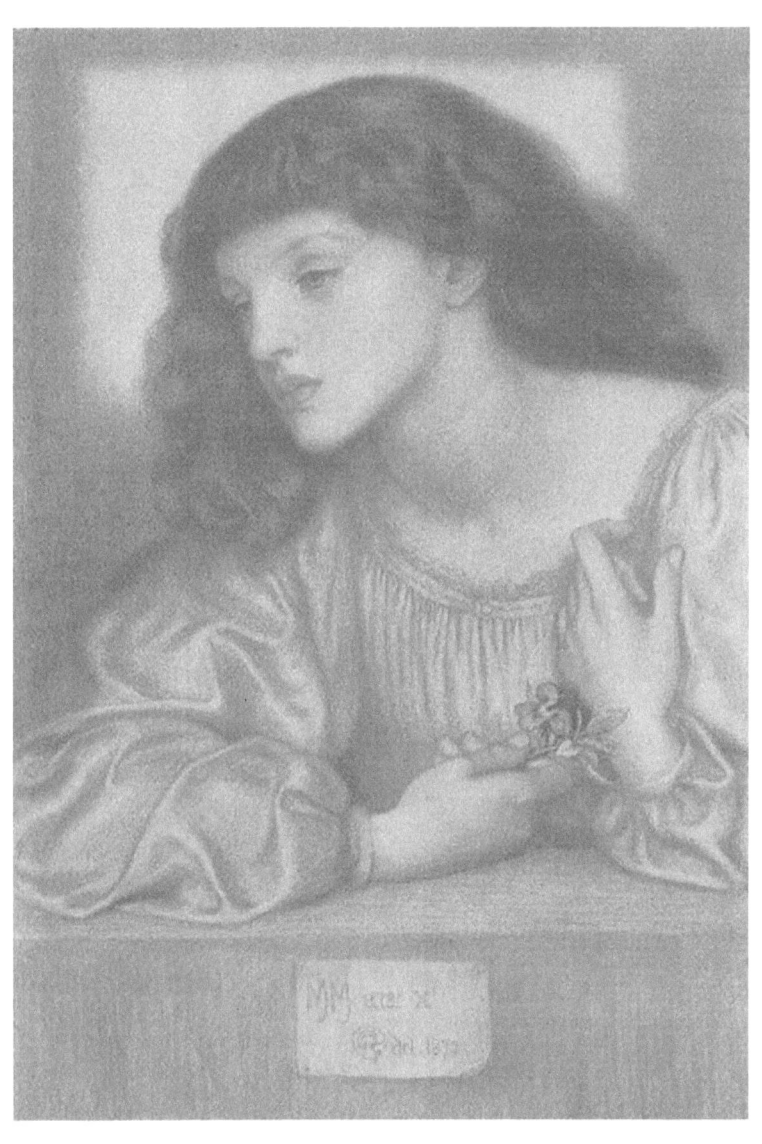

May Morris, 1873

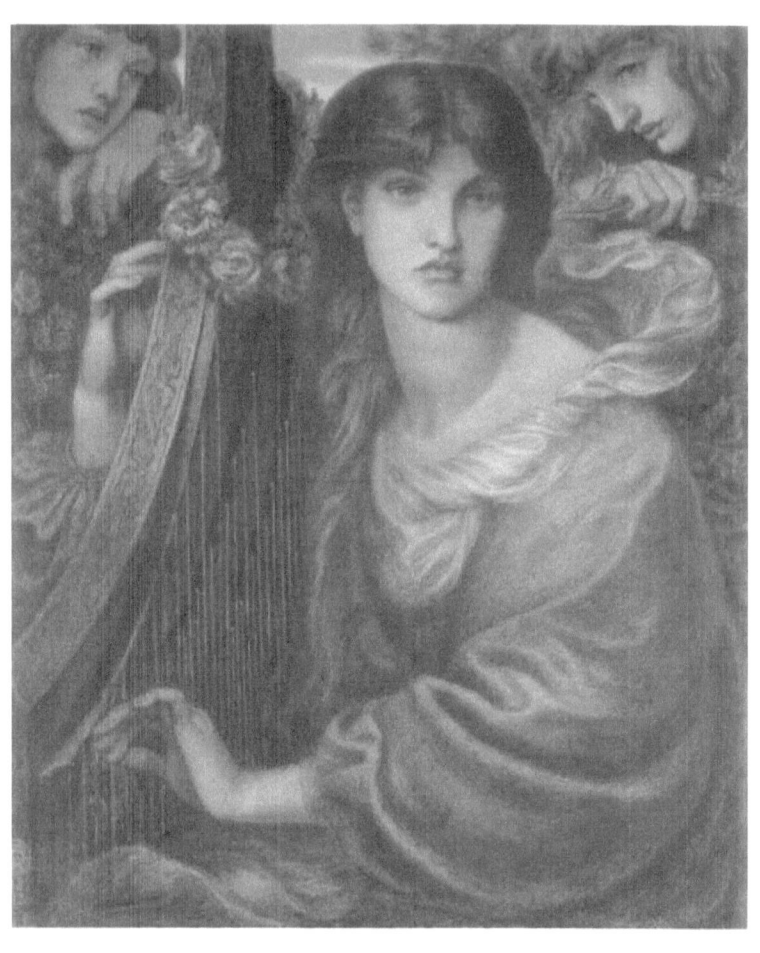

La Ghirlandata, 1873

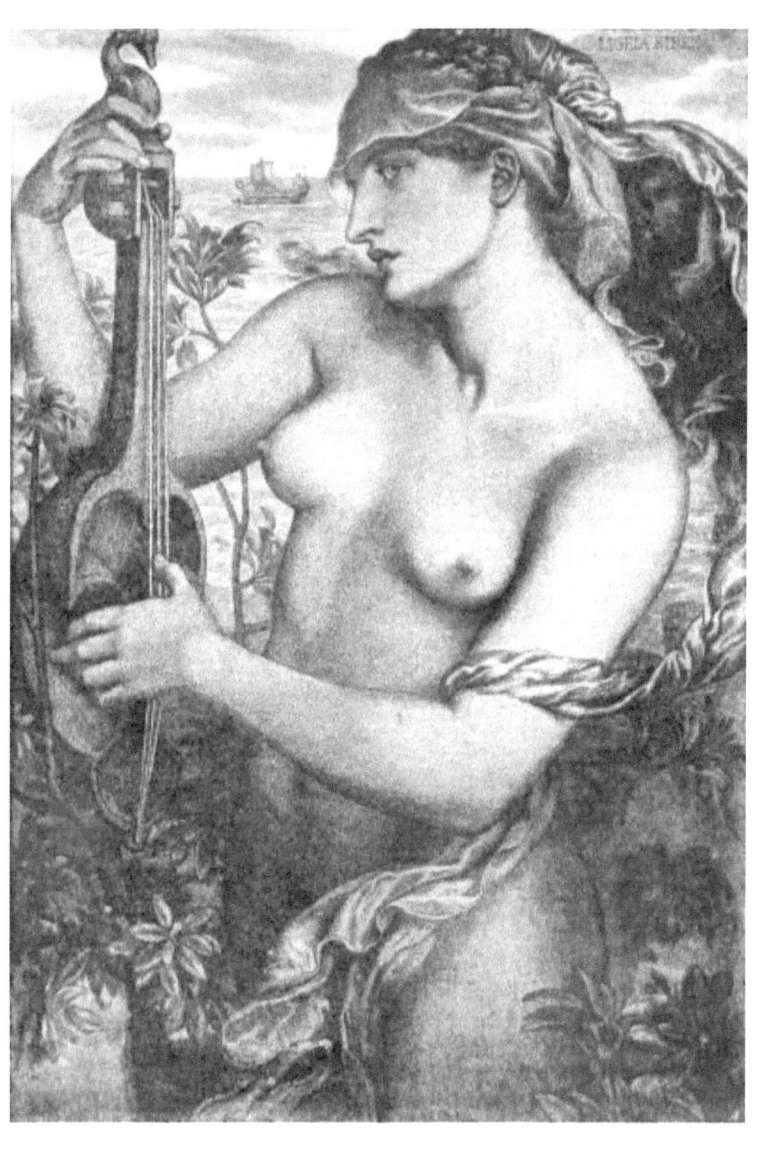

Ligeia Siren, 1873

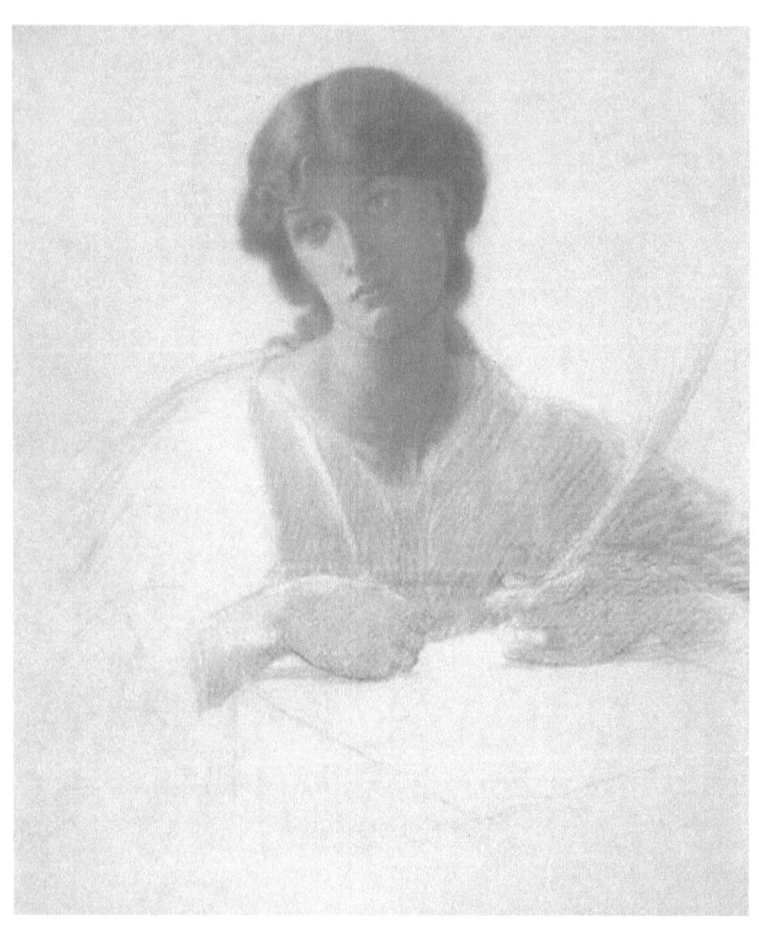

Study for 'The Blessed Damozel', circa 1874

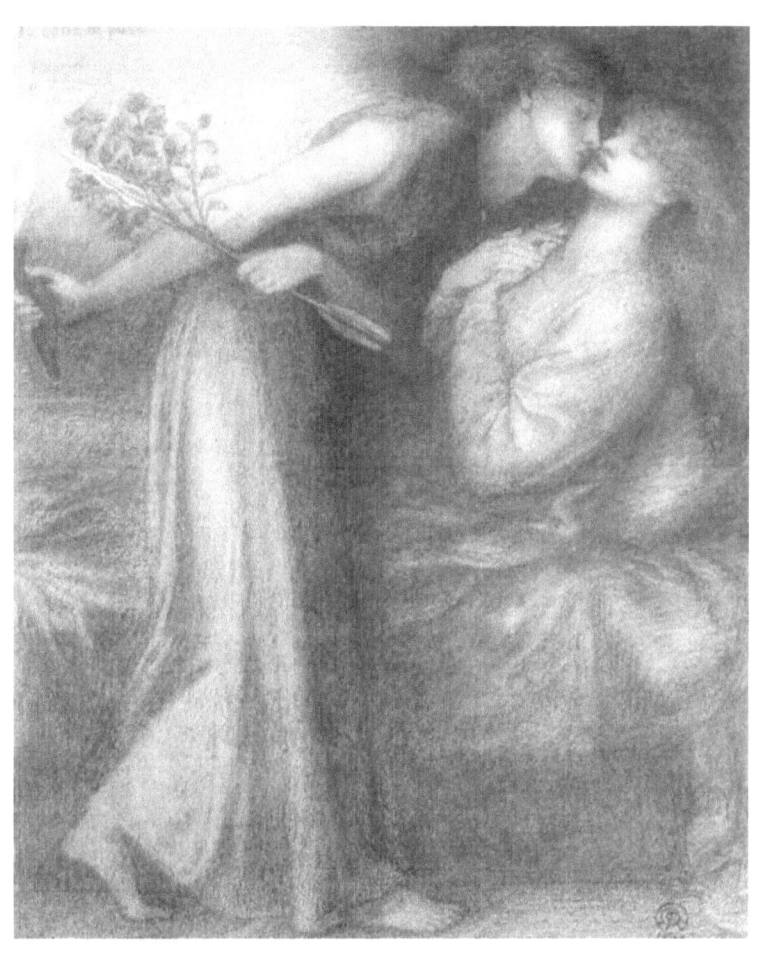

Io Sono in Pace, 1875

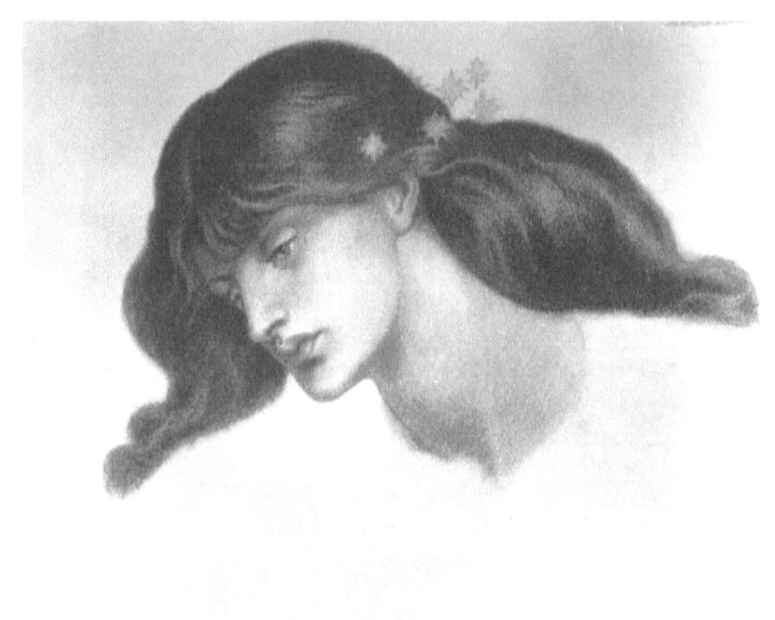

The Blessed Damozel - study, 1876

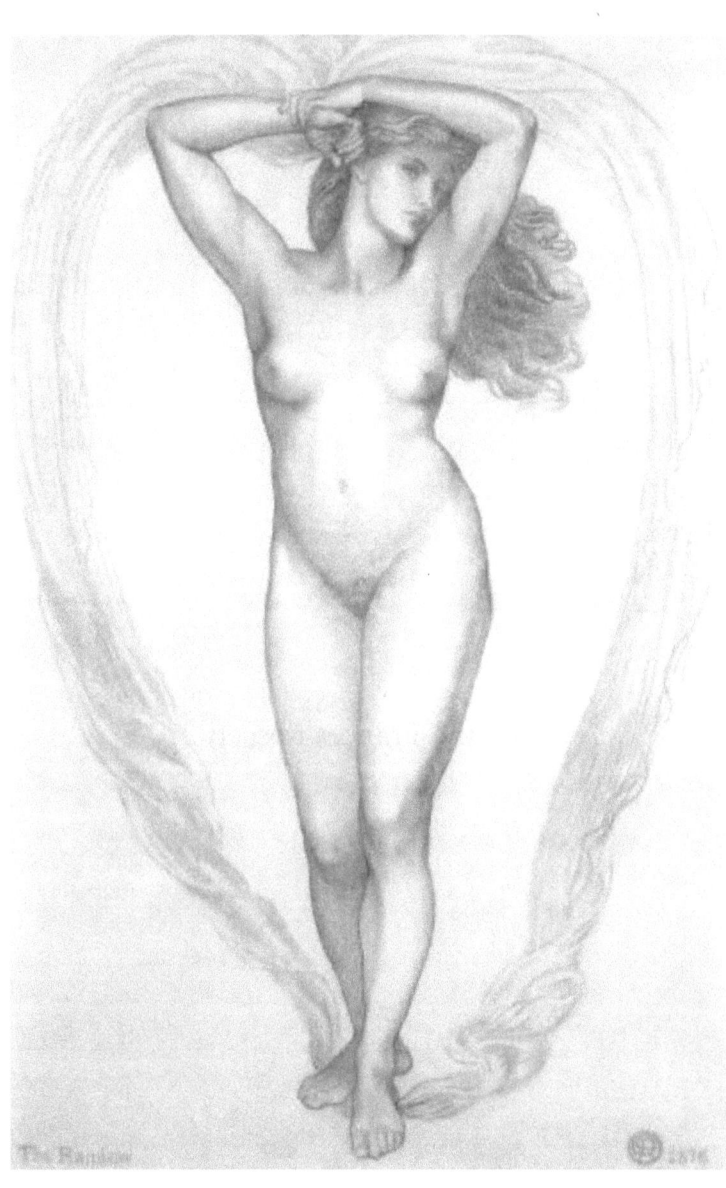

The Rainbow, 1876

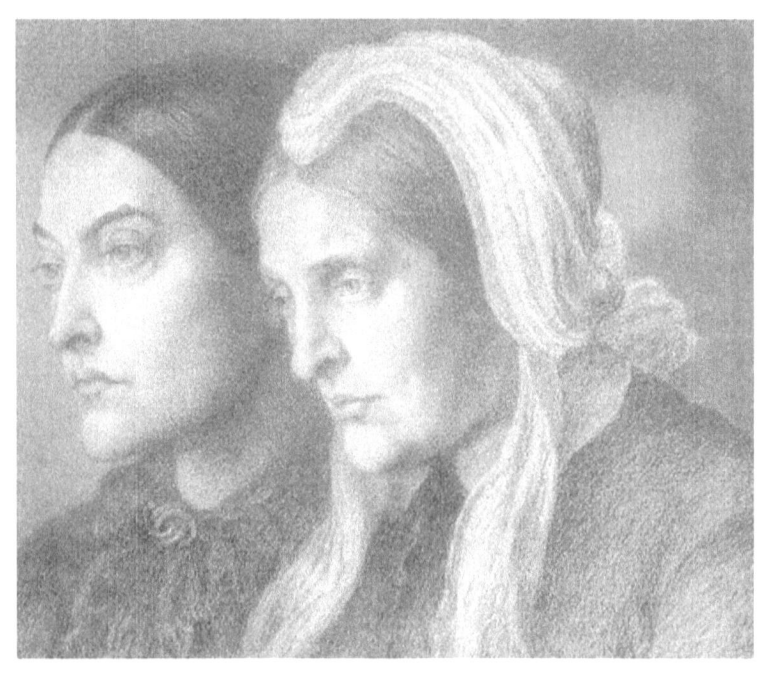

Christina and Frances Rossetti, 1877

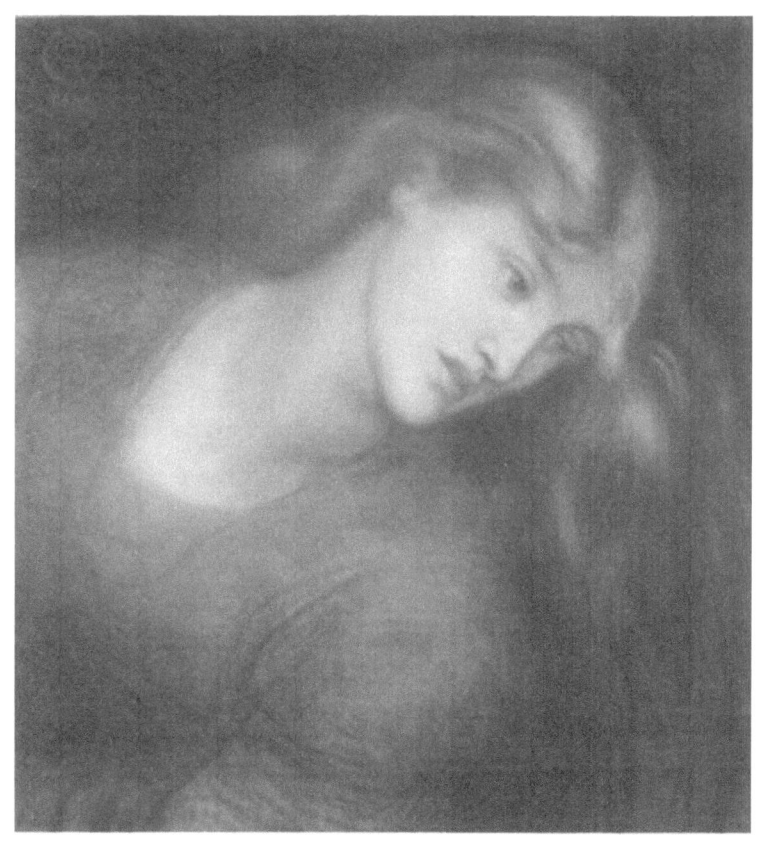

Aspecta Medusa, 1877

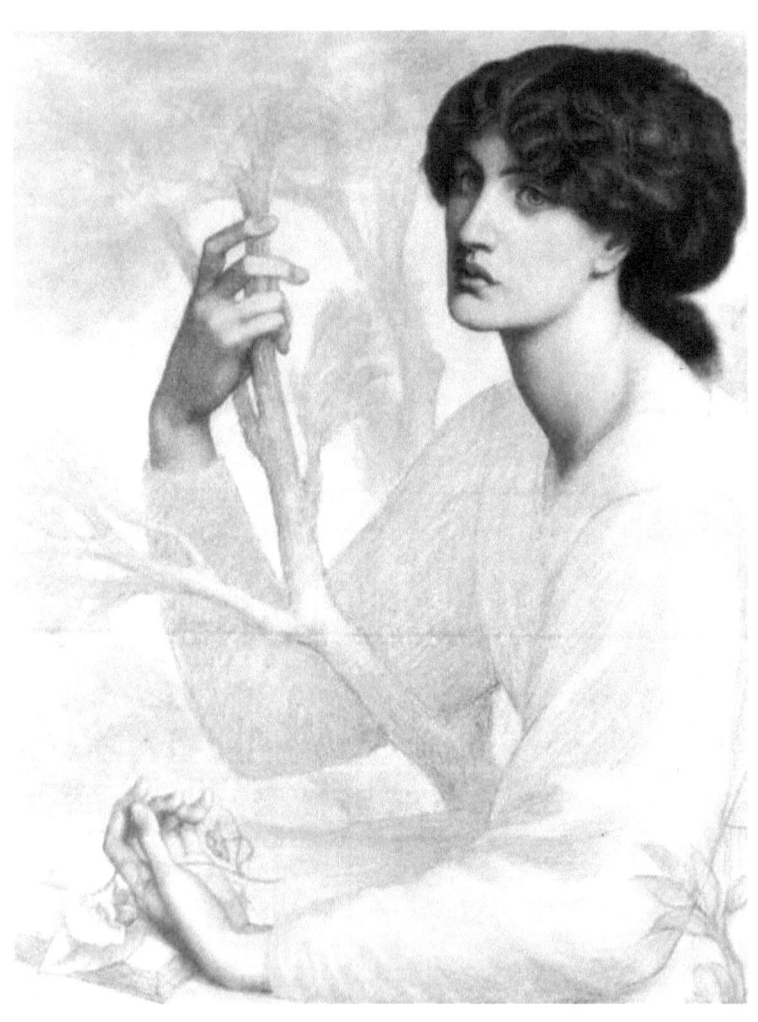

The Day Dream - study, 1878

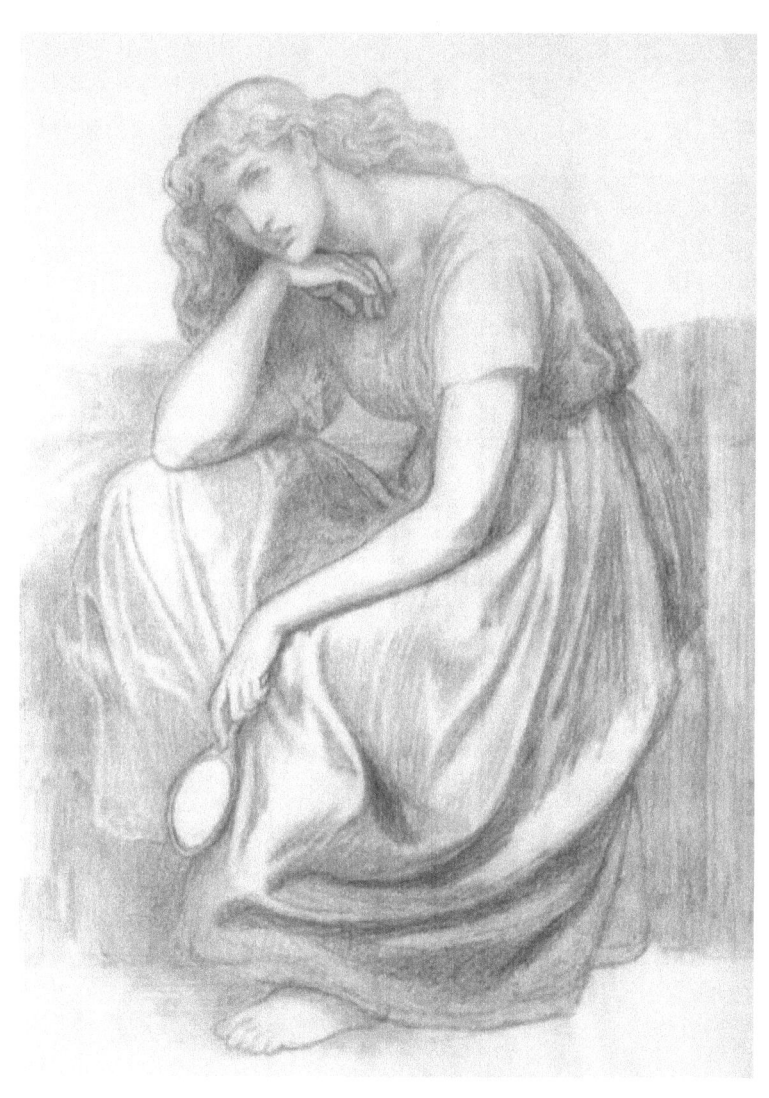

Desdemona, circa 1878-1881

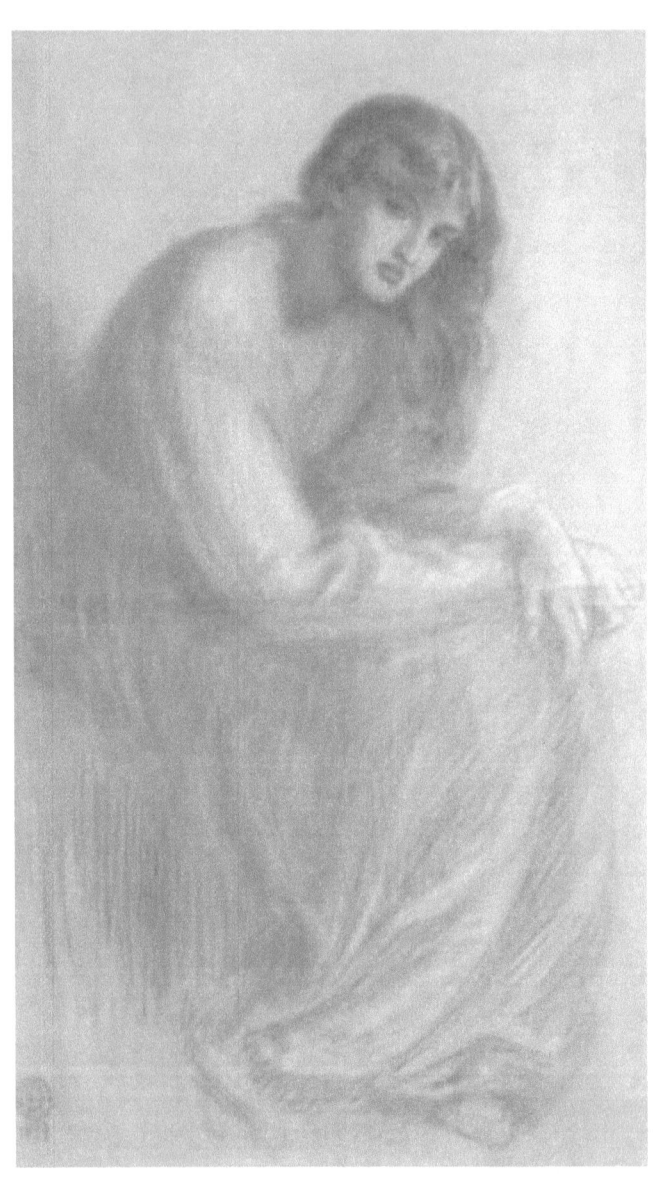

Alexa Wilding, 1879, chalk

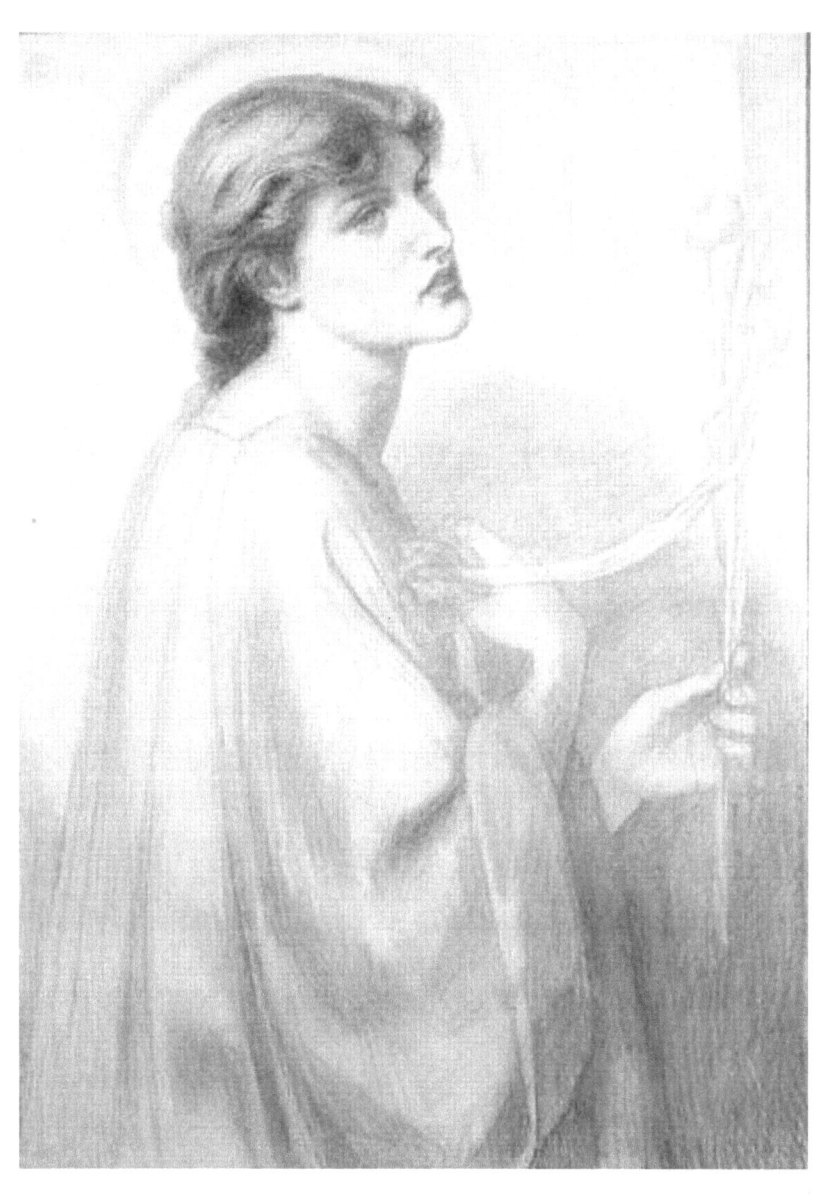

Sancta Lilias, 1879

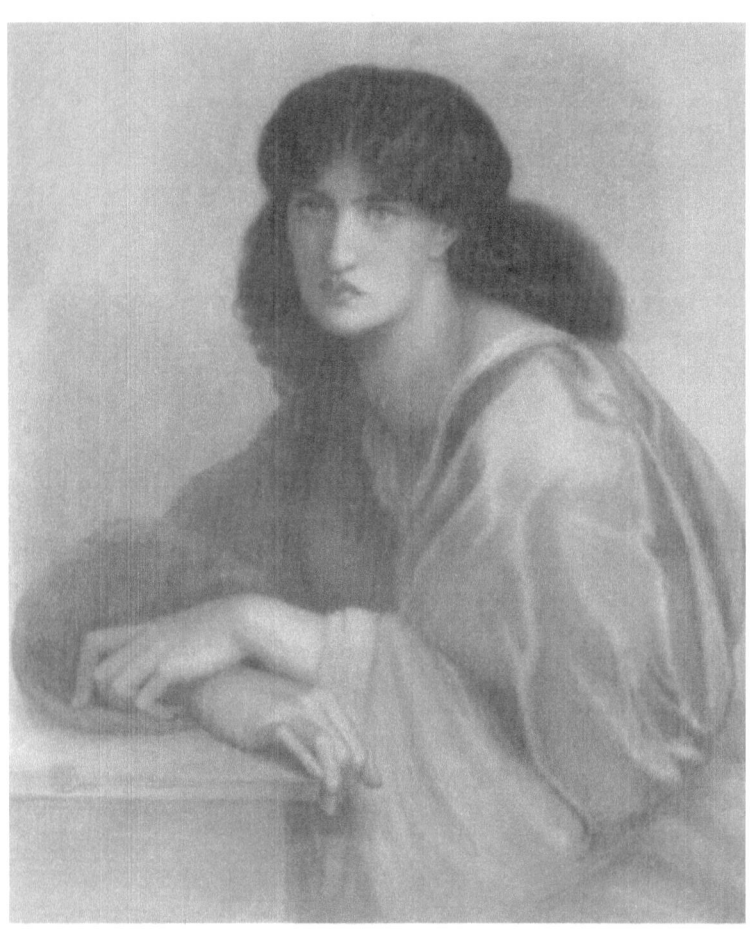

La Donna della Finestra (also known as Jane Morris),
1880

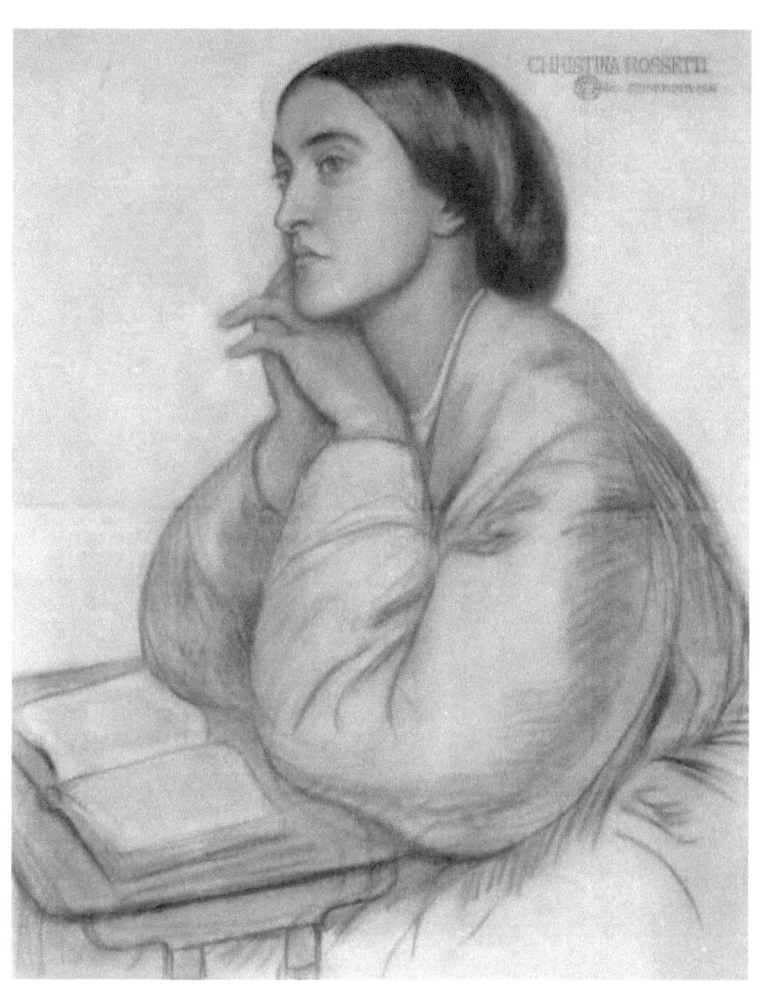

Christina Rossetti, 1886

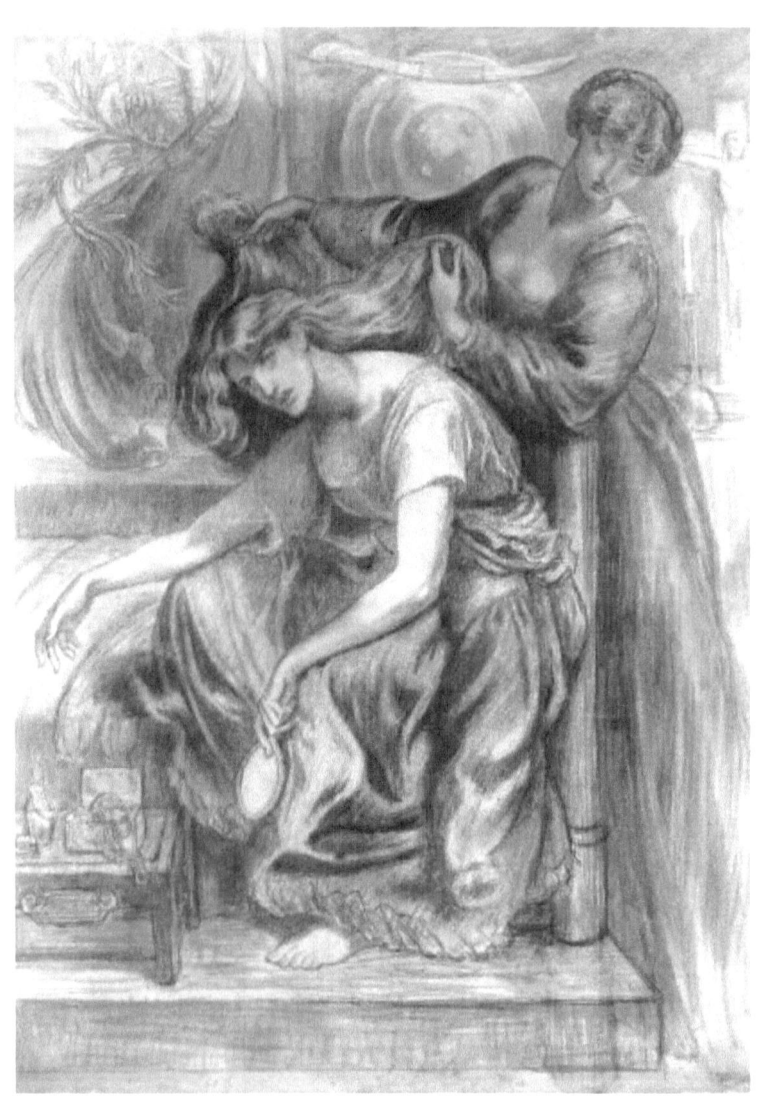

Desdemona's Death Song, Date unknown

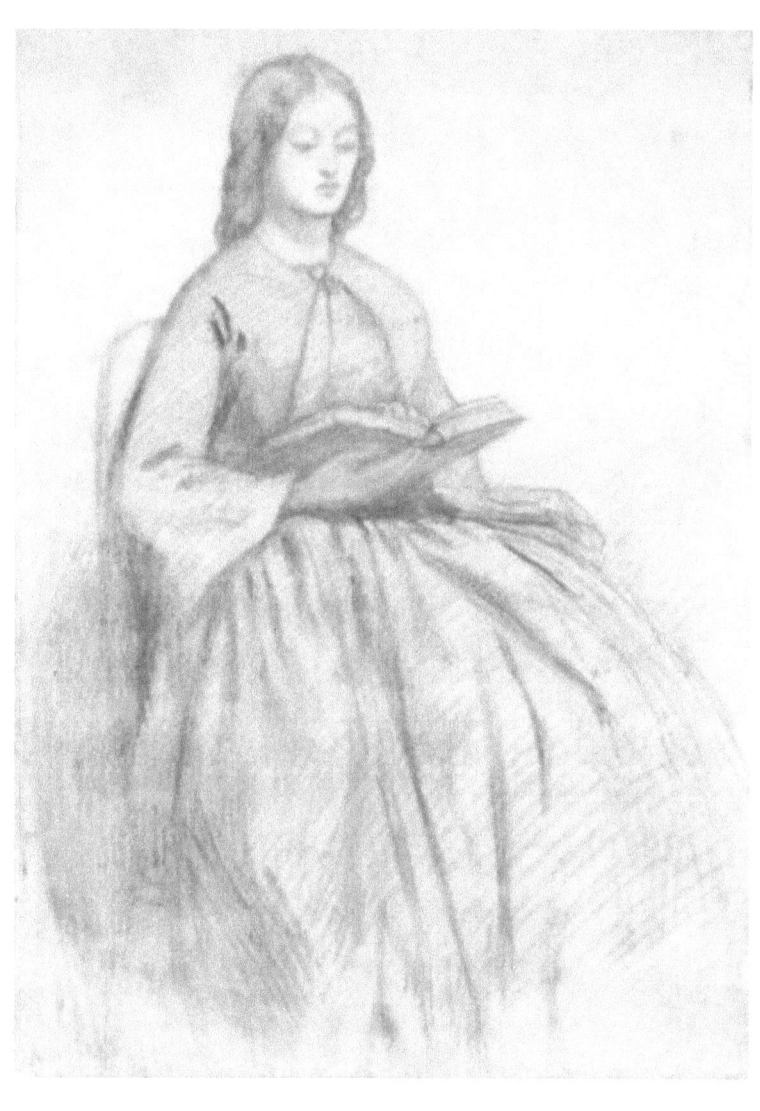

Elizabeth Siddall in a Chair, Date unknown

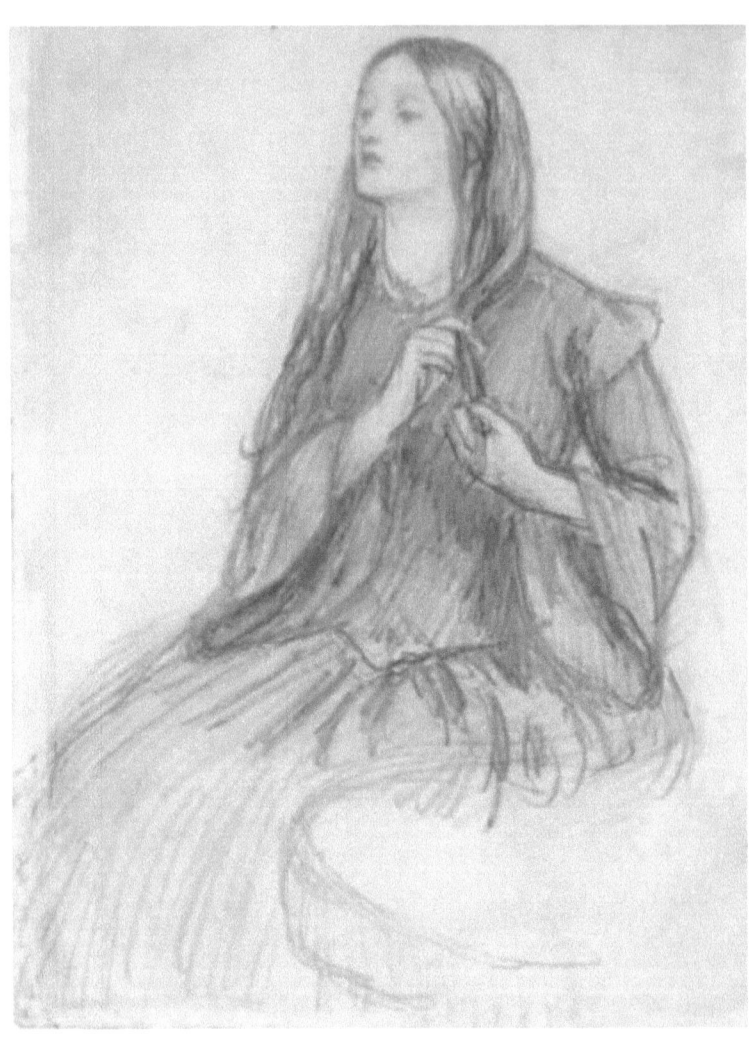

Elizabeth Siddall Plaiting her Hair, Date unknown

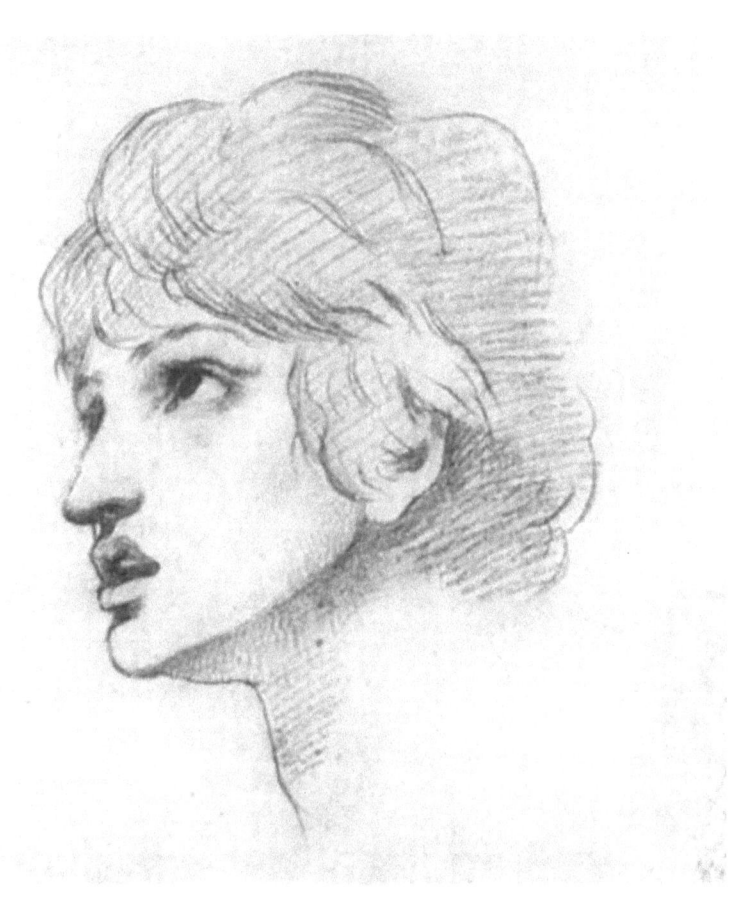

Head of a Youth, Date unknown

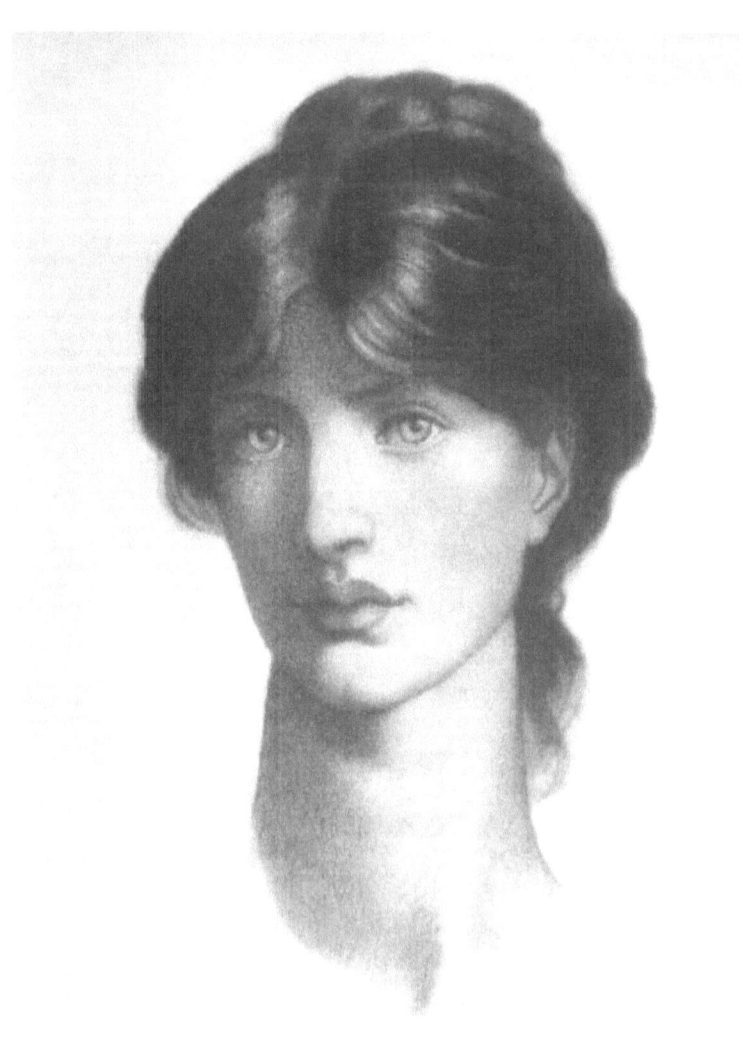

Study for a Vision of Fiammetta, Date unknown